NO ORDINARY MAN
William Anderson's Edinburgh Journal

COVER: High Riggs, Edinburgh, *c.* 1902

William Anderson, Elizabeth Anderson, David Ovenstone and Maggie Forbes.
Wedding, July 18 1902.

NO ORDINARY MAN

William Anderson's Edinburgh Journal
1903-1906

with a Canadian Epilogue

CITY OF EDINBURGH DISTRICT COUNCIL
RECREATION DEPARTMENT, LIBRARIES DIVISION

ISBN 0 900353 08 2

Printed by Macdonald Printers (Edinburgh) Limited
Edgefield Road, Loanhead, Midlothian

"No Ordinary Man":
William Anderson's Journal

INTRODUCTION

This *Journal* came into the possession of Edinburgh City Libraries in 1981 through the good offices of Alex Anderson, then Librarian of Heriot-Watt University. The Anderson family in Canada had sent a copy to Heriot-Watt University because of their father's connection with the College in 1904.

Knowing that the Edinburgh Room in the City Libraries collects a wide range of resources on Edinburgh and its people, Alex Anderson kindly arranged to deposit a copy with the Edinburgh Room.

Having read the *Journal* it was felt that with a suitable introduction and epilogue, it would make an interesting social document for publication. The Anderson family readily agreed to this proposal and to contribute an epilogue continuing the story of William Anderson in Canada.

Canadian Epilogue has been prepared by Olwen Anderson, William Anderson's daughter, and continues the story of his life in Canada. It is interesting that he pursued many of the interests in Canada, mentioned in his Edinburgh *Journal*, but unfortunately he worked such long hours that he did not manage to continue his *Journal*.

Olwen Anderson, like her father, obviously enjoys writing and has taken part in an oral history group in Toronto similar to *Prestonfield Remembers* and *Leith Lives*. In a recent letter she wrote that when typing for a scholar, who later became a Professor at McMaster University, she mentioned her father's *Journal* and its contents. The Professor-to-be remarked "Not many ordinary men kept diaries". Her reply was "My father was *no ordinary man*".

The story is presented as follows:

Edinburgh at the Turn of the Century: William Anderson's Edinburgh.
My Journal, 1903-1906.
Canadian Epilogue, 1906-1942.

Edinburgh at the Turn of the Century: William Anderson's Edinburgh

In 1903, Edinburgh was a city of 413,000 inhabitants covering an area of almost 11,000 acres, with Leith still a separate burgh with its own Provost and Town Council. Various public works had been recently carried out—the North Bridge, Waverley Station and Waverley Bridge being completely rebuilt in 1897 and the North British and Caledonian Hotels opened in 1902 and 1904 respectively.

Public transport had been improved with the introduction of cable trams in 1898, the suburban railway, opened in 1884, providing a service between 5.30 am and 11 pm daily, and cars and lorries were not unfamiliar sights on the city streets.

Edinburgh's traditional industries of brewing, distilling, papermaking, printing, insurance and banking were flourishing and contemporary trades directories record many other occupations, which gave employment to the working population of the city. Unemployment was also prevalent and it had been necessary that year to make a plea to the Lord Provost's Committee of the Town Council, to provide temporary work for over 700 men.

During the 18th and 19th centuries the boundaries had extended considerably so that in the early 20th century, the city consisted of the historic Old Town, the Georgian New Town, villages which had been absorbed during expansion, industrial areas which had grown up along the line of the railways and the Union Canal, the developments on the Burgh Muir and suburban areas with a rural atmosphere.

At this time, the local press was reporting Mr Chamberlain's South African Tour, War in Morroco and the Delhi Durbar. Sales were advertised in the Princes Street shops of Greensmith Downes, Charles Jenner and Maule's. Edison's *Animated Pictures* were to be seen in the Operetta House in Chambers Street and Lord Balfour of Burleigh visited the city to open Leith Nautical College.

Against this background, William Anderson, a coalman employed by St Cuthbert's Co-operative Society wrote his *Journal*.

He had been brought up in Freer Street as a boy and had attended the Vennel School. It seems likely that before becoming a coalman he had worked in Howden's Rope Works. When he begins his *Journal* in February 1903, he was living with his wife Elizabeth Ann (Cook) Anderson, a Welsh girl, at 69 High Riggs. They had married in 1902 when he was 27 and she was 22.

Their home, just beyond the Old Town area was near the industrial area of Fountainbridge and Dundee Street. It was probably a modest house, rented at £4/12/0 per annum and simply furnished with the household goods mentioned in the *Journal*. As their family grew they moved to larger flats at 105 Dundee Street in April 1903 and 49 Fountainbridge in May 1905. Bill makes many references to the hard physical work involved in being a coalman, especially in frosty weather when the bags of coal were "like barrels". "Coop" carters were earning 28/- for a 54-hour-week in 1911, so in all probability, Bill earned even less in 1903.

He and Liz lived a very busy life particularly after the birth of their daughter Peggy ("Wee Mag") in 1903 and their son William in 1905. William senior obviously took his duties as a father seriously and refers constantly to helping his wife with the children and the housework.

Bill, however, was an active Socialist, politically aware and determined to "improve" himself by attending evening classes and guilds, reading widely and writing both poetry and prose, which were published in local magazines. All these activities, which caused his absence from home in the evenings, not unnaturally gave rise to domestic friction.

In a typical week, after rising at 5 am each morning except Sunday, and spending 54 hours delivering coal, Bill occupied himself in a number of ways. Usually at 10 am on Sundays he attended St Cuthbert's Young Men's Guild in King's Stables Road, where there was a talk on the scriptures. In the afternoon he and Liz took a walk with the children and visited relatives. In the evening he might attend a meeting of the Social Democratic Federation, held at the Mound or in the Meadows.

During the week he attended classes at Heriot-Watt College in English literature and composition (where he won a poetry prize) or classes in Lothian Road in book-keeping, arithmetic, economics and French. He freely admitted that he often fell asleep at his Lothian Road classes and it was only when studying English literature and composition that he felt in his true element.

He was a member of both the Sons of Temperance Friendly Society and the Ancient Order of Free Gardeners. He therefore attended meetings of both organisations and was himself a sick steward for the "Sons", which meant visiting sick members and paying them their dues.

He clearly appreciated the importance of reading and spent many hours in the public library in Dundee Street and at local bookstalls buying books to add to his own collection. On Thursday evenings he attended the Literary Section of St Cuthbert's Young Men's Guild either debating such subjects as *Who is Better Off—Employer or Employee?* or reading his essays on William Cobbett or Robert Fergusson.

Not only did he work on debates and essays but he also contributed regularly, both poetry and prose, to *Echoes*, a monthly, published by St Cuthbert's Co-operative Society, and to *Town Crier*, a monthly Socialist periodical, the official publication of the Carters. *Town Crier* was first published in 1903 and the *Journal* contains several references to meetings with the editor and to Bill and other young Socialists actually delivering copies of *Town Crier* in the Stockbridge area.

Apart from these regular weekly activities, Bill and Liz enjoyed special occasions like their annual week's holiday in July, when they had picnics at Cramond or Portobello. Along with 1800 others, they went on the annual "store" (St Cuthbert's Co-operative) outing to Arbroath or had an occasional treat of a 6d seat in the Lyceum or Empire Theatres.

Bill's lighthearted comments on events in the city such as the Royal Visit in

1903, Baillie Waterson's funeral, the Royal Review in 1904 and Miller and Richard's band playing in the Grassmarket, mirror reports in contemporary newspapers, but give the events additional significance as he was an eyewitness and often wrote articles for publication afterwards.

His musings on unemployment, the nationalisation of the coal industry, the demonstration of Trades against the Trades Disputes Bill and Lord Rosebery's Free Trade Meeting, although not of great historical significance, are spontaneous and reflect the thoughts of someone who was *involved*.

Even on the first page of his *Journal* he showed an interest in emigrating to Canada, although he was dismayed after seeing the Canada Agent, to learn that wages were 10/- weekly and board. Unfortunately there is a gap in the *Journal* between December 1905 and June 1906, when Bill took the momentous step of leaving Edinburgh for Canada, and we do not know what led up to his decision.

After describing the voyage to Canada, the *Journal* ends with Bill starting his job with Massey-Harris in Toronto in June 1906. His *Journal* leaves us with a cameo of a working family in Edinburgh in the early 20th century, but we have to rely on his family to tell us what happened to Bill and Liz in Canada.

MY JOURNAL

William Anderson,
69 High Riggs,
Edinburgh, Scotland.

1903
Thursday
Feb. 12

"I have this day made up my mind to keep a Journal. I take this hint from Wm. Cobbett, whose *Advice to Young Men* I am at present reading. . . ."

Taken from the diaries at present in the hands of Gordon Anderson, grandson, of Cobourg, Ontario.

Typed by Olwen Anderson, daughter, of Toronto, Ontario.

November 1981.

FAMILY TREE

William Anderson   *b.* May 2, 1875   *d.* November 19, 1942
                       Edinburgh, Scotland   Toronto, Canada

Elizabeth Ann Cook   *b.* December 14, 1880 *d.* October 3, 1959
                       Ysleferra, Wales   Toronto, Canada

Married—St. Cuthbert's Church, Edinburgh,
Scotland. July 18, 1902

Children

Margaret Forbes   *b.* May 23, 1903
                       Edinburgh, Scotland

William   *b.* June 7, 1905   *d.*
                       Edinburgh, Scotland   "buried in single
                                               child's grave, Prospect
                                               Cemetery, January 5,
                                               1910: aged 4 years, 6
                                               months"

James Cook   *b.* December 23, 1907
                       112 Dufferin Street
                       Toronto

Rheta Elizabeth   *b.* January 14, 1911
                       99 Armstrong Avenue
                       Toronto

Frederick William   *b.* April 14, 1913
                       78 Empire Avenue
                       Toronto

George Laing   *b.* April 14, 1913   *d.* October 4, 1959
                       78 Empire Avenue   Toronto

Llewellyn Francis   *b.* August 12, 1917
                       166 Cedarvale Avenue
                       Toronto

Olwen   *b.* November 19, 1919
                       27 Empire Avenue
                       Toronto

2

MY JOURNAL

William Anderson,
69 High Riggs,
EDINBURGH

1903
Thursday
Feb. 12

I have this day made up my mind to keep a Journal. I take this hint from Wm. Cobbett, whose *Advice to Young Men* I am at present reading. I think Cobbett was a genius of the first water; and have made up my mind to become better acquainted with him through the medium of his books.

We are at present living in a small house in 69 High Riggs (rent £4:12). We last week bought a plain chest of drawers for 8/-, a bargain. We also last week got a nice room table from Mrs. Innes.

Sunday
Feb. 15

This morn I got up and went to the Guild Meeting where a fine paper was read by Mr. Wilson on *The Mission of the Twelve* (Matt.10). In the forenoon I went to Gollogly's where Ned, Jim and I had a talk about Cobbett, religion and education. I think it is most instructive to talk on a good subject with people who understand it.

In our class this afternoon, Miss Robertson talked on Interpretation, taking the Butler's and Barker's dreams from Genesis and Joseph's interpretation of them as an illustration.

Monday
Feb. 16

There are lots of men who think it a feminine action for a man to do housework. This I think a weakness as there is no better way of showing the woman you love and who loves and suffers a lot for you, your love, than by helping her with those little household duties.

Spite is a dreadful thing and the man who has a spiteful nature has an enemy that will rob all the pleasure out of his life. I hold spite against no man.

Sunday Feb. 22	During the latter end of last week I have been half entertaining an idea of going to Canada. All I need is the resolution and the money. It is a strange thing to think that the resolution of a minute may bring about the condition of a lifetime. What a great thing chance is. I remember coming down Lauriston Place going home to Freer Street, when I began to ponder should I come down by Lauriston Street. I did so, and met Ned and Jim with whom I was standing talking when Mary Ann Gollogly came along with a young lady to whom she introduced Jim, Ned and me. That young lady is now my wife. So much for the small chance of just coming down Lauriston Street.
Sunday March 1	Today I was going down the High Street when I saw a little girl leave her little brother and go and pick up a crust of bread that was lying on the street. I couldn't help feeling sorry for her as she devoured it—perhaps many a dog had sniffed it and scorned to eat it—I gave her a copper asking her what she would buy with it. "Sweeties," was her reply. Some people prefer luxuries to necessaries. I made her promise to buy biscuits before she went away in high glee.
	I sent in a piece to *Echos* today. The Store sale.
Sunday March 8	Today I went to Guild at 10 a.m. where we had two papers and some remarks from Rev. Mr. Craig on *The Confession*. The papers were by Messrs. Walker and Wilson. I spent the evening in Mr. Goodwood's lodgings where I had tea and supper with him.
	The evening before, Mr. Goodwood had a certain amount of work to get through. He worked strenuously to try and finish it before 12.00 a.m. His fellow-lodger sat with the watch in his hand and prompt at 12 a.m. stopped Goodwood, who was going in good form. So much for strict Sabbatarianism. Another hour and he would have finished it. I think Goodwood an ideal Christian and think he will yet become a great man.

4

Monday March 9	I went to the Library this evening—also Gollogly's. I have been thinking of how the putting off for 'just one day' that which we would rather not do and consequently the thing never is done. I have no doubt the world has lost many a good thing just through putting off.
	Today I have taken out Bunyan's works from the library.
Friday April 4	Two months ago I bought this book with the intention of every day writing some small thing down. The various dates will show how I have neglected that little job. And yet this is only one instance of good intentions and plans not being fulfilled. There is too much "Oh, I'll do that some day soon," but that some day never comes. When you make up your mind to do anything, every effort should be made to do it. Let nothing keep you back. This is good advice, but I can't act up to it.
	Last night I visited Mr. Hadden. Then went to the last meeting for the session of our Guild. In the election of Office Bearers, I was appointed Delegate to the Church Council.
Saturday April 4	Today I have the toothache bad. I went to bed in the afternoon. It being no better in the evening, I found it necessary to go round to the dentist's and part with that tooth and one shilling. It was an inch long. (The tooth—not the shilling).
Sunday April 5	I went around to Gollogly's in the afternoon. Arranged with Jim and Ned to take up the study of French. In the evening I attended the Annual Conference of the Young Men's Guild. Met Lizzie, Lydia and Mr. and Mrs. Macintosh with whom I had a short walk.
Monday April 6	Tonight I went round and had my first lesson in French. Previous to that we went up to Aitken's sale and bought a mirror for 2/6 and a wringer for 4/6.
Tuesday April 7	I was up to Mrs. Cockburn and the library. We had a visit from Maggie Forbes and Davie Ovenstone, and John Young. It spoiled my night at French.

Wednesday April 8	Lizzie and I went to Mrs. Cockburn's, who was ill. We, later, had visits from John Young, David Ovenstone and Davie Ovenstone.
Wednesday April 8	Had walk with Jim and John in afternoon. French with Jim and Ned in evening. Today St Cuthbert's opened a new coal station at Corstorphine. The first day's work amounted to twelve bags. It will be interesting to watch the growth.
Thursday April 9	Cockburn's at night with L. G.'s later where I had a half-hour at French then a walk with Jim and Ned.
Friday April 10	Good Friday. Concert at Free Gardner's Institute (Sons of Temperance). First concert.
Saturday April 11	Jim's in afternoon and had a turn at French. In evening had walk out with Liz and Mr. and Mrs. Macintosh. Had David up in evening.
Sunday April 12	Infirmary at 9 a.m. to see Mrs. Innes. This being Easter Sunday, we (Lydia and I) went to Church and took Communion at the afternoon service. In afternoon, I went down to see Mrs. Cockburn. Class at 5 p.m. Mrs. Gilbertson's in the evening.
Monday April 13	Jim's in evening for French in which I am progressing slowly. Walk with Jim and Ned later.
Tuesday April 14	Ditto.
Wednesday April 15	Went along to Mr. and Mrs. Lawson in Horne Terrace where my wife and I had a most enjoyable evening.
Thursday April 16	Lizzie and I went to Mrs. Cockburn's, then library, then Aitken's sale. Afterwards I went to Jim's for French. Short walk later. Had visit from Mary Finney from Maitland Street.
Friday April 17	I did a big lesson in French in evening and went round to Jim's.

Saturday April 18	Walk along Fountainbridge with Liz and met Mr. and Mrs. Macintosh with whom we had a walk down Cowgate.
Sunday April 19	I went into Infirmary to see Mrs. Innes, Lizzie's late old landlady. She had died that morn at 1:30 a.m. She was in her eighty-eighth year. Gilbertson very ill. I was round to Gollogly's in forenoon. Class at 5 p.m. Visit from Mr. and Mrs. Walker in evening.
Monday April 20	Holiday. Mr. and Mrs. Macintosh and my wife and I took the car for Portobello and walked from there to Niddry to see Mr. and Mrs. Laurence Martin. We had a most enjoyable day and were home at about 8:30 p.m.
Tuesday April 21	Went to see the last of poor old Mrs. Innes and was invited to the funeral which was private. Had visit from Mrs. Chandler, then went to Forbes's where Liz was.
Wednesday April 22	Went to Mrs. Innes' funeral in afternoon at 3 p.m. In the evening, I accompanied Mr. Lawson his round lighting lamps, round Blackford district. He then came home with me when he, his wife and we had tea. This morning, Tom Gilbertson died. Poor Tom! I met Ned at breakfast-time and went up and saw Tom. I was very sorry. How uncertain life is. Just the other day, Tom was one of ourselves. He was every ready to oblige. He was the friend of many and the enemy of one—himself. Poor Tom! If you have sinned you have suffered. My heart hopes you have been forgiven and that you have met a merciful God.
Thursday April 23	Went up to Mr. and Mrs. Innes to see about buying some of their late mother's furniture: fender, washstand and tubstand. I went up to Gilbertson's later for about an hour.
Friday April 24	Jim's at 6:20 p.m. Afterwards to Innes' where we paid for the tubstool, washstand and fender.

Saturday April 25	Mrs. Innes sent for me to come and see about the purchase of the room chairs, sofa and a bed. I hurried home at 2:20 p.m., got changed as quickly as possible to go to Gilbey's funeral at 3 o'clock to Grange Cemetery. Was home again at 4:20 p.m. Went a walk with Liz. In the evening, I went up to Gollogly's then to Cockburn's, then library, then Aunt Lizzie's where my wife was. Home at 10:20 p.m.
Sunday April 26	Did not go out during the day. In the evening, Liz and I went to Forbes's.
Monday April 27	Mrs. Innes' in the evening when we removed some things to our new house at 105 Dundee Street.
Tuesday April 28	Again shifted some things to our new house from Mrs. Innes'. Also helped to pack up chest of drawers which was going to Gateshead.
Wednesday April 29	We drew for our holidays today. I drew June 8th to 13th, inclusive. Went up to Mrs. Innes' in afternoon and gave carryman a hand to take down the drawers. In the evening I went along for Jean Nelson who visited my wife while I gave my Aunt Lizzie a call. My mother came home from Newcastle.
Thursday April 30	Mrs. Innes' in the morning at 5:30 a.m. when I removed a lot of rubbish into the street. In the afternoon, I shifted the last of the many articles we bought and got from young Mrs. Innes.
Friday May 1	In the afternoon, I heeled my wife's shoes and toed my own boots. Then went up to Forbes' with Lizzie's small box.
Saturday May 2	My birthday. Twenty-eight years old today! Getting on Bill! In the afternoon, Liz and I went to Finlayson's. In the evening I was down at Gollogly's new house.
Sunday May 3	I did not go anywhere until 5 p.m. when I went to class Then to G.'s. Later, Liz and I went to Forbes'.

Monday May 4	Liz bought me a new cap for my birthday. I went to library, then to Cockburn's in the evening. Later, Liz and I went to Macintosh's. It was a very wet night.
Tuesday May 5	In the dinner hour today I went into Robertson, Atholl Place, to have some repairs done to our new house at 105 Dundee Street. In afternoon I went up to Finlayson's for Liz where she was working. In the evening, I visited John Young from whom I got photo, and Mrs. Forbes. Afterwards, we had Mr. and Mrs. Macintosh and Mrs. Gilbertson up to supper.
Wednesday May 6	I went to the funeral of Mr. James Dawson, one of our old workers. Poor old James, a done old man at only fifty-four years. In evening I met J. Young and took him into our new house to show him our sofa which he was going to repair. Later, we went to Archie Thomson's and bought some cheap floorcloth.
Thursday May 7	Visit from young Mrs. Innes. After that, I went along for J. Young who came and sorted our sofa.
Friday May 8	Went with Gibson to "Sons". On the way home, met Mr. and Mrs. Mack, whom I brought home with me.
Saturday May 9	Splendid day. Had walk along Princes Street in afternoon with Liz. The Town is partly decorated in honour of the King and Queen who are to visit it next week. Aunt Lizzie's with Liz and Mr. and Mrs. Mack in the evening.
Sunday May 10	Was not out all day until evening when I went to class. Forbes' later with Liz.
Monday May 11	G.'s a short time in evening. Mack's with some of our things later.
Tuesday May 12	Wrote some verses and paragraphs for new paper *Town Crier*. Mack's in evening.

Wednesday May 13	Met Tom MacDermott at 8 a.m. and went with him to funeral of a shopman who died at South Side. What a contrast. The streets were all finely decorated in honour of the King who was on a visit here. And we solemnly patrolled through all this gaudy grandeur with our dear fellow-worker behind.
	In the forenoon (this was a holiday), I was round at G.'s. In the afternoon, I stationed myself at the foot of High Riggs and saw the King and Queen passing. In the evening, Liz and I want to Forbes'. I returned alone.
Thursday May 14	Liz along in morning again. Tom McD. gave me a hand along to our new house with some things. Later, Liz and I went to Forbes' where Liz stayed.
Friday May 15	My first real bachelor's day. In the evening, I went to Cockburns, then library, then to Forbes', where again Liz stayed.
Saturday May 16	In the afternoon, Liz and Nelly Forbes came along. I went along with them to Forbes'. Home myself at 10:30 p.m.
Sunday May 17	Up at 8:00 a.m. Read and wrote till about 2 o'clock. Then went to Forbes'. Had short walk and called into Mack's with Lizzie. I was home at 10:10 p.m. Wrote "Martin's Got a Laddie".
Monday May 18	Gave D. Miller lines on the death of his wee boy. He was greatly touched on my reading of them. Had walk with Liz and Nelly Forbes in evening. I was at G.'s earlier.
Tuesday May 19	This day was observed as the King's birthday holiday. I went up to the High Street to see the procession. Met the G.'s on way up. In the afternoon I had tea at Lydia's place. Forbes' later to see Liz with whom I had a short walk.
Wednesday May 20	Lydia came home in afternoon and cleaned up house a little. I wrote to McUrtin. Neddy and I went to Cockburn's, then to Forbes'.

Coronation Arch, Lothian Road, *c.* 1903. *By kind permission of Trevor Yerbury.*

Thursday May 21	Liz came along and tidied up house for me. We called in at Mack's. Mack came home with me and took away bedchair, I taking the baby-chair.
Friday May 22	Letter from Mr. Robin. In the evening I went to house factor (Robertson), then to Finlayson's, then to Forbes'.
Saturday May 23	This is a most important day in my life. It being the occasion of our first born's arrival. A little girl, born at 1:45 a.m. in the house of Mrs. Forbes at 88 Temple Park Crescent. Everything passed off satisfactorily. Mrs. Mack also had her first born, hers being a boy. Today I saw an old woman, seventy-two years, lying on the street at Dalry Road. The poor old soul had been knocked down by a motor car. She died in an hour. The driver, aged nineteen, was taken into custody.
Sunday May 24	I went along to Forbes' in forenoon. Liz doing very well. In afternon I called in at Mrs. Mack's and Aunt Lizzie's, also visited Mrs. Cockburn whose son, Johnny, died the preceding Friday (May 22). His wife had died the same date four years before. Poor Johnny! There is one sad heart mourns your unhappy fate. I hope you have met a merciful God. I then went up to our Aunt Bella. My Uncle was lying very ill. Forbes' again in evening.
Monday May 25	Forbes' in afternoon. In the evening I packed up some books for flitting, Forbes' later. Liz getting on finely.
Tuesday May 26	All bustle packing up for removal. Allen's lorry came at 9:30 a.m., and took the furniture to 105 Dundee Street. I passed the night in 1 Gibson Terrace.
Wednesday May 27	I got my meals in Robertson's. Shifted along remainder of things. Then went to Forbes'.
Thursday May 28	Forbes' at night.
Friday May 29	Forbes' at night.

Saturday May 30	Mrs. Robertson's, then Forbes' in afternoon and evening.

Sunday May 31	Still living in Gibson Terrace. Sleeping on a bedchair and feeling very lonesome and miserable. Robertson's for breakfast, then Forbes', then Robertson's again for dinner and Forbes' again for the rest of day.

Monday, Tuesday, Wednesday,
Thursday, Friday & Saturday

Forbes' every night during week. Liz was visited by Mrs. Robertson on Thursday. On Friday, Liz got up a little while. Liz again up and feeling stronger on Saturday.

I got into our own house on Tuesday of this week.

Friday July 17	By the day we are one year married. We had Mr. and Mrs. McDermott, and Aunt Lizzie and Cousin Bella to tea in the evening. We all enjoyed a nice quiet time.

Saturday July 18	By the date we are one year married today. Our baby is eight weeks old. In the evening, Lizzie and I went up to Lydia's place. A walk later.

Sunday July 19	Nell Forbes in afternoon. Band in afternoon at 6:30 p.m. Met Mr. and Mrs. Strachan on the Hill.

Monday July 20	Wrote to the *Clarion*. Had Tom and Mrs McDermott along, Also N. Forbes.

Thursday Sept. 17	After a lapse of nearly two months, I again return to my 'daily' diary. Today we had a post card from Dave and Maggie Forbes who are both in South Shields for a holiday. We had the baby vaccinated. Some time ago I had a lecture all to myself from Dr. Farquson on the benefits of vaccination. For all that, I still think it a brutal assault on innocence. Each day as I see our darling baby suffering so unnecessarily—to my mind—I become more and more of an anti-vaccinator.

In the evening I went down to Guild and gave one shilling for subscriptions for Leslie B. Dalgliesh. I am now on the Guild Committee. I am also recording scribe for the Sons of Temperance. I was thinking of dropping out of the Free Gardeners but resumed paying last fortnight.

Friday Sept. 18	I have just finished reading Blatchford's *Book About Books*. It is splendid. I am now starting Smiles *Self Help*.
	Our baby is very cross tonight: partly owing to her teeth and partly the vaccination. Some doctors say that the babies never feel any pain. Do the little darlings cry and let their tears flow copiously just for fun, I wonder? I feel convinced they do suffer and a good deal, too. Do doctors think we are fools when they are telling us such utter rubbish? If they were amputating a limb from Lord Sneezum without chloroform, would they tell him it would not hurt? I'm afraid not, or their fees would be also hurt.
Saturday Sept. 19	In the hope of doing something for the Guild, I foolishly took on the writing of an essay on William Cobbett. I wonder if I would have been doing the Guild a greater sevice by not writing it? I wrote to Mag. F. and Dave. In the evening I accompanied my faithful spouse on her commands and returned as usual "tired and heavy laden".
Sunday Sept. 20	"A day of Rest." Perhaps. I was up first—I always am—made the usual brewing of tea, tended the fire, nursed the baby a little, fires again, baby again, and so on. I have now a few minutes which I am using up on my diary. Visit from Mr. and Mrs. Forgie, R. D. Walker.
Monday Sept. 21	This is a "holiday". My wife is washing and I am her labourer, when I am not nursing, I am working the wringer; and when I am not working the wringer, I am nursing the baby. Between the two I am very busy. A holiday. I'd rather be working for a rest. Wrote lines on the departure of Leslie Dalgliesh. Sent them to Cairns. Had walk with wife in evening. Holiday over.

Tuesday Sept. 22	On Saturday last, a young man bravely attempted to stop a pair of runaway horses that were in a C. R. lorry in Princes Street. He was knocked over and killed. At his funeral which took place yesterday, his father interrupted the priest and said, "Down with him: down with him. The dog!" He was shown out of the cemetery by one of the gravediggers. It is a terrible story and makes me wonder are such men human.
	Tonight we had a record number of visitors. Five women, two men, a boy and a dog. I would sooner have ten women than that dog again. What an animal! When it was not barking it was jumping on our knees or hunting through the press. I will still continue to welcome and entertain friends, but dogs—never!
Wednesday Sept. 23	Some time ago I got the loan of a book from a friend. I lent it to a friend of mine and went up to his house and got it, with a view to restoring it to its original owner. What a good job my friend had not lent it to another friend, who in turn might have lent it to his friend, and—well, there is no saying how far it could have gone.
	Later I went to the Coalmen's Mission meeting. A young man preached from John III.16. He may be very earnest but he is no preacher.
Thursday Sept. 24	With my usual diligence, I lost the Son's of Temperance Roll Book some time ago. I am writing out another. In the evening, I went to our Guild where our Ex-President, L. B. Dalgliesh received a present of a golfing set on the occasion of his departure for So. Africa. I wrote some lines on the occasion. They were well received on my reading them. I accompanied Mr. Cairns home. During the evening I signed my name as seconder in favour of "Municipal Trading".
	"Well, Tommy," said a proud father to his young son home from school. "How did you get on today?" "Oh, Father, I got dux for natural history. Teacher asked how many legs a horse had and I said five." "How did you get dux for that. You were wrong." "Yes, Father, I know, but the other boys said six. I was nearest it."

Friday Sept. 25	My sister, Annie, had her first-born today—a boy. She was very ill and had chloroform. In the evening I went to the "Son's" meeting, where I found the Officers' Roll Book, and during the meeting took the minutes.
Saturday Sept. 26	The afternoon was wasted in the usual manner, reading a bit of this paper and a bit of that paper. In the evening, Liz and I went out together. She was in an awful state because I had not shaved. She behaved in a dreadful manner; so much so that I lost my temper and expressed myself rather strongly. There are limits to human endurance. Still the man that gives way to temper is a fool and much to be pitied. We had Mrs. Forbes and Mrs. Strachan in in the evening.
Sunday Sept. 27	In my usual vocation of nurse and fireman. Wrote my minutes. Then I went to Mrs. Hadden's with a jam tart from my wife. In the evening, we went up to Forbes' and then all—Mrs. F., Lydia, Nell, Liz and I had a walk along Princes Street.
Monday Sept. 28	I wrote some points down in favour of Municipal Management. It must be admitted at the same time that there are flaws in Municipal Management. For instance, the Engineer of the Edinburgh Gas Works has 1,500 pounds a year. A fabulous sum which our worthy Provost wants to be increased. In the evening, I went to the Hope & Forgie Lodge where I spent a most enjoyable evening.
Tuesday Sept. 29	There is a very good saying of Abraham Lincoln's: "You may fool some of the people all of the time, and all of the people some of the time, but you can't fool all of the people all of the time." I went to Cockburn's and the library. Later, I met the G.'s in Melbourne Place.
Wednesday Sept. 30	In the evening, I was at a loss where to go and decided on spending the evening and three pence in Poole's Myriorama. Some years ago, I was thinking of buying a Chamber's Encyclopedia but spent the money on a pair of books. They serve the same purpose for they improve my understanding.

Thursday Oct. 1	*Town Crier* out today. I have for the third time in four tries won a prize in the poetry competition. Some time ago, an editor said I was going backward with my poetry. This does not look like it. A friend of mine says the woman he marries must be silly and rich. Rich to make him take her and silly if she takes him. If ever I marry again—Heaven forbid!—I will make but one condition with the bride. She must be dumb. None know better than married men the truth of that beautiful saying of Carlyle's "Speech is silvern: silence is golden".
Friday Oct. 2	Some years ago a man expressed an idea that all workers in Britain and Ireland should strike. What a silly idea. I imagine I see every street and lane that leads to the Workhouse thronged. The British Workman is only five days from the Workhouse at any time. How very insecure is the workman's position. Never sure of the possessions he has toiled a lifetime for. Out of work, illness or kindred misfortune and the rich man will come clamouring in for his seventeen ounces of flesh, and sell the bed on which you may be dying from under you. I know of one instance of this. The man who caused it for some petty debt was an elder of a church. Pious man! Would Christ do that? Miss Robertson's social in the evening.
Saturday Oct. 3	Of all my departed friends, the one who appears oftenest to my mind is Thomas Gilbertson. It takes me some time to realise that Tom is really gone. Poor Tom! A more genuine or true heart never beat in the breast of man. Yet your departure from this life was not a great sorrow. So much, dear Tom, for the cursed influence of drink. A good intention—and you had many of them—is no use without a strong resolution. In the evening had the usual walk with Liz and baby.

17

Sunday Oct. 4	It rained all through the night and morning. At about 12 p.m. today a poor, half-dead cat dragged itself in at our open door. On being put out of the kitchen, it came into the room. Poor beast! I put it into the coal closet and tried to make it take some warm milk. It could not take it. On looking in again in the evening, it was dead. Its back appeared to be broken, evidently the work of some savage dog. Perhaps set on by no less savage a master. I had almost said man. Our class started today at 5 p.m., when Miss Robertson gave a lesson from Moses. I got an invitation to Mrs. Robertson, St. David's Terrace for Tuesday night. In the evening, Liz and I were at Forbes'.
Monday Oct. 5	In the evening, I went with Tom McDermott to Lauder House, Jeffrey Street (Pickwick Club) to hear paper by J. M. Hogg (Young Scots) on Social Reform. Tom put a question to him and another member of the S.D.F. pointed him out on a few things. It came out at 10:40 p.m. In my hurry home, I took the longest road home (Princes Street) for a short cut. Just like Bill—full of mistakes. My first one was made at my birth. My second one when I was at death's door when a baby of six weeks. I didn't die.
Tuesday Oct. 6	A fearful day of rain! In the evening, I went to Robertson's, St. David's Terrace. There were a good few hymns sung during the evening. There is a beautiful feeling pervading in a Christian home. Such as an atheist could not but admire and envy. They are poor in wealth but rich in spirit. The son played on a small organ and everything was sacred. I remember reading on a wall: "Two things are impossible. First, to make people better. Second, to make people worse."

Published on the First of Each Month.

The Official Organ of the Carters' Association.　　A Journal devoted to Labour and General Matters.

No. 2, Vol. I.]　　　　ONE PENNY.　　　　[JUNE, 1903.

Leith Town Council and Their Carters.

TUESDAY NIGHT'S COLLECTION.

The longer an industrial dispute continues the more embittered do the relations become between employers and employed.

A lengthy discussion took place at this ... Council relat... ...sociations ...

believing in the necessity of efficient civic administration, instruct their Secretary to send a communication to the Town Councils of Edinburgh and Leith, respectively, sug- ... an official Gazett... b...

THE TOWN-CRIER.

Welcome The "Town-Crier.'

A hearty welcome, Mr. Queen,
I give your splendid magazine;
It is the best that I have seen,
　　　　And 'twill improve.
I hope your fellow-carters mean
　　　　To make it move.

Let the "Town-Crier" aid procure,
'Twill fill a long-felt want, I'm sure;
I think it will success endure,
　　　　It well deserves it.
Your power to help the carters' poor,
　　　　You won't reserve it.

God strengthen you to bring success,
The carters sorely need redress;
Though some's not worth it, I confess,
　　　　Still fight on, pray,
And may your labours ne'er grow less
　　　　From day to day.

　　　　　　　WILLIAM ANDERSON,
Prize of 2s. 6d.　　69 High Riggs, Edinburgh.

If you have a good joke to tell, write it down and send it along, addressed—"Joke Competition," "␣␣␣ Crier" Office, 3 ␣ ␣␣reet, L␣␣ ␣he 15␣␣

rier.

:RS.

sent by post
advance of
␣; or 1s. 6d.

..ld be ad-

.., to be made
.-Crier."

ication must
'r only.

others are
'ef, bright,
␣ chance of

..urned unless
enclosed.

.mpetitions ex-
s by special

Each ␣
must encl
coupon wil.
the competi

COM?

No. of Comp
Name........
Address..
　　......
Date......

Hawick

It will be
the carters
tion with
increased ␣
Saturday
instead o
inclusive.
settlement
␣n advance

Poem by William Anderson printed in *Town Crier*.

19

Wednesday Oct. 7	How the days roll on, then the months, then the years and so on the lives of men. I take a backward look over the years gone by and incidents of many years ago seem happenings of but yesterday. I intended going out this evening but alas! "The best laid schemes, etc." My wife declared otherwise. Our home is like unto a ship of which she is the captain. The baby is first mate and I am the crew. I am under the stern rule of a stern feminine hand. What a lot I always intend doing. As a contrast to that—how very little I get done.
Thursday Oct. 8	There is a popular fallacy that to get wet the water only gets to the skin. This is silly—it is when it gets past the skin that rheumatics set in and makes old young men. "Good-bye, William," said the dying ma-in-law to her son-in-law. Previous to that she only called him "Bill". "Good-bye, I'll meet you in Heaven." And since that day Bill has stopped going to Church. In the evening, I went to Mrs. Cockburn's with a letter which I wrote to her son in U.S.A. She was very pleased with it. The surest way to win a woman's affection is through praising her family and the surest way to win the affection of the family is by praising the mother. So to be popular, praise everybody.
Friday Oct. 9	Cobbett tells a story of the most drunken wretch in his regiment who would go home without any money and get over the difficulty by "calling our ugly brat of a kid a most beautiful angel."
	In taking the minutes of the meetings now I find it much easier. Tonight I was appointed reporter to the Sons of Temperance at a salary of nothing a year, payable in advance. I am like a journalist out of work for I have no copy. I am looking for some supposed interesting matter to inflict on the long-suffering British public.
	My wife's breast is very sore today, as also is her arm.

Saturday Oct. 10	My wife went down to the Dr. this afternoon. He said she was not very bad as she had caught the evil in time. He told her to go home and treat it and he would call again tomorrow. The treatment cost about 6d. I expect the superfluous visits will be 7/6. Of course, the wealth-producing working man can easily pay it. What would a man do with his money if it were not for those exceedingly obliging persons coming in and removing some of it—or all of it—occasionally. Aunt Lizzie's in the evening.

Yesterday I got a needlecase as prize won in *Town Crier* Rhyme competition. Even editors blunder! What does a man—a poet, too—want with a needlecase? Some hairpins is liker his want.

Sunday Oct. 11	Liz very bad with her breast. Mrs. Forbes came in the afternoon as also did the Dr. I went to class at 5 p.m. Miss Robertson talked on "The Plague in Egypt". It struck me as rather rough on the Egyptians that the plague should visit them through the stubbornness of Pharoh. I think, but of course I am uncultured, that God should have dealt with Pharoh direct. Job is a character in the Bible whom I much admire. The man who can control his temper and at the same time nurse a crying baby also commands my respect. His patience is a virtue very surely.

Fools laugh heartiest at their own folly.

"It is very strange how my hands are so cold in the winter and not in the summer," said one of our old men.

Monday Oct. 12	On Thursday last I was in Mrs. Gilbertson's. How I missed Tom from the house. How his family is growing! Soon everyone will be working and helping their most deserving mother. The girls, Kate and Barbara, were going to a night school. This is a step in the right direction and I was glad to see that they were anxious on it. In the evening Liz and I went to Bella Forsythe's birthday party. Liz's breast was much better. Home at 11:45 p.m.

Thursday Oct. 12	The 15th of each month is the last day for receiving matter for the *Town Crier*. I just manage to get mine's in on that date. Tonight I sent away some verses and other matter so that he would get them on the 14th, a day earlier than the limit. I have taken a note of this wondrous fact. "Procrastination is the thief of Time." This might be improved on. "Procrastination and women are the thieves of Time." One half of women's time is wasted with dressing. The other half is wasted while they put on their hats. Mr. and Mrs, McDermott were here in the evening.
Wednesday Oct. 14	What an overpowering thing sleep is! Tonight I went with two friends to an economics class, and despite my hardest efforts, I could not keep awake, and dropped the book out of my hand. I started up and blushed shamefacedly. The lecturer is talking from Blatchford's *Britain for the British* and his arguments besides being instructive are very convincing. This I picked up while I was awake.
Thursday Oct. 15	In the evening, I visited the G.'s and debated several things including religion, municipal trading, and co-operation. Afterwards, I went to the Guild, then Dundee Street Library and home.
Friday Oct. 16	The man who has two masters has much work but the man who has a stern mistress is worse off indeed! Tonight, like a faithful follower and attendant, I went with my wife to do shopping. When I was tired carrying the baby, the wife took her and gave me a parcel twice the baby's weight to carry for a rest. I afterwards visited the G.'s for the evening. I got a letter from the *Crier* editor asking me to come to a meeting to discuss the improvement of the *Crier*.

Saturday Oct. 17	Out in the afternoon with wife and baby. Visited G.'s, then went shopping. This evening, I went up and saw my sister's little son in its death throes with convulsions. Poor little thing! How the little face would twitch and the little chin drop and there would issue from the little open mouth a weak shriek. It was cold all over and it was only its very strong heart that was keeping it alive. Three times during the day had its eyes been closed by my Aunt under the belief that it had passed away! Three times, however, were they deceived and the little mouth would twitch again and the tiny scream come forth. The little darling passed away to a sweet rest at 11:15 p.m., aged three weeks and one day. Needless to say, my sister and her husband are much grieved with their loss. They have our sympathy.
Sunday Oct. 18	This morning I went up and saw my sister's dead child. How sweetly it was laid out. There lay Wee Archie after his very brief stay on this earth. He looked what he really was—a perfect little angel. What a beautiful thing is death in a child, yet how hard it is to console a mother to such a fact. They say it is better away then suffering. But I say it is better away whether suffering or no. What is there in this world for the offspring of working people to grow up for? Nothing but misery, and hard knocks, and hard working for a living or rather a starving. Man's life in the working classes is not enviable. The child that dies young is the luckiest child born.

There's not much between death and mirth after all. Last night, while my little nephew was drawing his last few breaths, the people next door were laughing and singing. Truly, I cannot think of a thin wall separating two such scenes. The one waiting on death's visitor with women weeping, and the other with people indulging in revelry as if care were a thousand miles away. Surely an ill-matched pair.

Annie and Logan were down to our house for the greater part of today. Mr. Hadden came in for tea. Later we went to Forbes'.

Monday Oct. 19	I hurried up with my work today and was done at 3:10 p.m. Home and got ready for baby's funeral which was timed for 4:30 p.m. Rev. Mr. Ross conducted a nice service and came to the funeral. Annie's later and I then went to Free Library.
	There are some people one finds very difficult to ask a favour from. Our present foreman is one of these. He invariably grants it, but previously takes the good out of it. The best way to avoid this unpleasantness is never to ask him for a favour. It is very hard to please everybody. The man who tries, even to his own disadvantage, will find in the end that he has not even pleased himself.
Tuesday Oct. 20	What a long face some men can wear when they are listening to the blessed doctrines of Christ on a Sunday. Yet you will often see those same individuals on a Monday morning rounding on some unfortunate persons who may be under them. This type of man is plentiful. Their Christianity has a fine surface but no depth. Tonight, Mr. Hadden and I went to a meeting of *Town Crier* contributors convened by the editor, Mr. Queen. Various forms of improvements were discussed.
Wednesday Oct. 21	Last Wednesday, I fell asleep at the economics class. Tonight I will again fall asleep but it will be in bed. When the body is fagged the mind won't work. Today I saw a little fellow who had been sent a message. His mother, thinking him rather long away, came down to look for him. She saw him a few yards from the entry. "Come away, come away! What's keeping ye?" But instead of coming, he started going, for he had been playing at the stairfoot all the time. I remained indoors this evening. This is a change indeed.

Thursday Oct. 22	"Boys will be boys," Say some folk when any boy has got into mischief. I take exception to this, as mischief and various evils do not constitute a boy. If it did, what would we term a very good boy? When a clock is wound up it goes best. When a business is wound up, it goes no more. "What a nuisance teeth are," I heard an old wife say. "They are a bother getting them, they are a bother keeping them, and they are a bother losing them." The man who came to sort our fireplace is a grate worker. When a man is knocked down, he is much upset.
Friday Oct. 23	Yesterday an old woman said ours was the youngest baby she ever heard saying "Dada". Of course ours is the most wonderful baby in the world. Ours is first. The rest are a dead heat for second place. They say the good die young. Of course, there are exceptions. Myself for instance. I went down in the evening and saw Tom's wife who was ill. Sons of Temperance later.
Saturday Oct 24.	A stitch in time saves nine. This does not apply to a stitch in the side. In the afternoon, Liz and I went down to McDermott's. Mrs. McD. is improving in health. The Municipal Elections are coming on. One of the main questions is 10 o'clock closing of public houses. One of the men in favour of it was recently locked in the municipal wine cellar, helplessly drunk. What a victory for temperance!
Sunday Oct. 25	The year is drawing to a close. How like a human life is a year. January 1st being its birth and so on it goes through its various stages till December 31st sees its death. This forenoon, I took the baby with me to see Mrs. McD. I also visited my Aunt Jean. This is my first since my marriage. They were all quite taken up with our baby.

Monday Oct. 26	I attended a musical concert lately at which a descriptive piece entitled "Waterloo" was played. It began with the airs of different countries: English, Scotch, Welsh and Irish, then French, then a lot of thundering on the big drum, firing of pistols and raising of red lights. I was thinking of going over to count the dead after it was over. The big drummer killed quite a lot. In the evening I went to a Municipal Election meeting for Welsh.
Tuesday Oct. 27	Some time ago, in my thoughts, I compared life to a voyage at sea—by-the-bye. I'm often very much at sea. We start away happy in its smoothness but we must look out for there are rocks. These are numerous in the working man's voyage. The most dangerous rock is debt. Beware of it, for many a promising voyage has come to an abrupt finish through that dreaded rock.
	Tonight we were to go to Forbes', Liz, baby and I. As it was pouring rain, only I went. Today I had a very nice letter from Mr. Stephenson, London.
Wednesday Oct. 28	What a lot of misery is self-inflicted. Lots of people through temper cause themselves and others endless misery. This is especially the case with lovers who fall out and adopt the "I-won't-speak-first" method. As a general rule, however, they speak and unfortunately, poor things, get married.
	Tonight I fell asleep over a book to which the author did not put his name—wise judgement. Did not go out. Was in bed early.
Thursday Oct. 29	Tonight I went up for Mr. Cairns to accompany him to Guild. Met him on Meadow Walk and he went back to ease his mother's mind by telling her that he had a friend with him. What an enviable thing it is to know that you have a mother's love. I am only thinking this, as I never myself experienced it. I have seen it in others, and that is how we gain knowledge in what we see in others and what we hear others say.

Friday Oct. 30	This evening I intended going to the Free Gardeners' Meeting. I went to G.'s first and was detained there at a party (Hallowe'en). During the evening I had an enjoyable talk with Mr. P. Welsh on books, and while the others were enjoying fun of a boisterous nature, we were enjoying ourselves more in a quiet way. I came away at 11 p.m.
Saturday Oct. 31	Liz went out in the afternoon herself. I went out myself. Went to library then had a walk around the book stalls. I am fairly in my glory among books. Were I a man of means my first hobby would be books. I would go to a bookstall and purchase his stock and most likely my wife would call in some other bookseller to purchase them back in the course of the next day.
Sunday Nov. 1	I was up early this morning. Our Sabbath morning fellowship started this morning. Dr. Williamson addressed us on St. Paul whose life is to be studied during the session. On coming out, I went to G.'s; came home. Did some writing; and at 5 p.m. went to the class when Miss Robertson spoke on the Israelites leaving Egypt. It was good of God to release the Israelites but He acted roughly with the Egyptians of the many thousands of whom not a man was saved.
Monday Nov. 2	Disraeli once said there were three different kinds of lies. There were lies, damned lies and statistics. He might have gone a fourth and said politics. Tonight I attended two Municipal Election meetings, also visited Mrs. Cockburn. Had Ted Walker up.
Tuesday Nov. 3	Some time ago, I started saving up. In a short time I had about 14/. A month later I had about 2/6 which shows my capabilities as a saver-down and how weak I am at saving-up. At St. Cuthbert's Co-op half yearly meeting, prominent on the platform was Councillor Welsh. The next evening, we find him on the platform with a private trader. It is handy when one can shift on a moment's notice. Today is polling day for the Municipal Election. I voted for McArthy. He got in with a majority of twenty-two votes over Welsh.

Wednesday Nov. 4	Today I decided to attend a bookkeeping class held on Wednesday evenings. I accordingly went and along with other men showed how little I know of that necessary subject. I remember one Sunday morning years ago, my mother was frying a splendid panful of haddocks for the breakfast, when there came a lot of dirt down the chimney and filled up the pan. I may say this sooted the fish, but it did not suit us. My mother was mad and her chances of Heaven were considerably lessened by what she said.
Thursday Nov. 5	Tonight was the first night of the 25th Session of our Guild. It took the shape of a social evening and was very enjoyable. Lydia and I went together. Our baby is cutting her teeth now and is going through the usual troubles inflicted on innocent children by nature. She waked up through the night crying. Poor little creature! After all she does not trouble us much. In the mornings when I come in to breakfast, she is always lying kicking and laughing, with the exception of several mornings lately. She has been asleep through having her rest broken during the night.
Friday Nov. 6	Sons of Temperance in the evening. I was thanked for letter which I had put into *Crier* on "Son's" behalf. Coming home, I had to debate with three of them and tell them that drink was not the cause of all the poverty in the country. If drink is the cause of all the poverty, what is the cause of mine, whose door drink never enters? Perhaps the low wages accounts for it.

Saturday Nov. 7	This afternoon, Liz and I went down to see Mrs. McDermott who is ill. We cheered her up a bit. In the evening, Tom and I went and drew our dividends. Mines was £3.14.9, less 13/- put to our Share Capital. Was home at 7:50 p.m. and did not go out again as the baby was not well.
	The Princess of Wales is alleged to have said she hated any woman who said hers...(The Princess's) were not the finest children in the world. This is an instance of hate arising from love. She loves her children so that she kisses each of them before they retire for the night. What love! I wonder does she nurse them much? I believe a workman's wife has more love for one of her own children than fifty princesses have for all theirs. The sickening thing is the way the press takes up and makes much of such silly things as what those princesses say.
Sunday Nov. 8	I was just thinking this morning how soon will pass away another year. The first whole year of our married life which, taken all things, has been a very happy one—and so it is, years moving slowly yet go swiftly by. Our lives are like one short year of time which flies past and is succeeded by another generation. So it has gone on for endless generations. Our baby was ill through the night and cried a good deal at intervals. The German Emperor in a toast to his sons recently said, "The help of God and of the Saviour, and to this let us fill our glasses." A rather curious toast indeed!
Monday Nov. 9	Our baby is much brighter today. She passed a quiet night. In the evening I had a long talk with Wm. Brodie, the Liberal snob. He said that no man willing to work need go idle. The fact that seven hundred men made application where only seven were required seems to knock that in the head. That's saying nothing of hundreds driven to suicide through want of work.
Tuesday Nov. 10	Baby in her usual health and cheery. Had visit from Ted Walker in the evening. A Jew once lost half a crown. In looking for it he found a half sovereign. "Mein Gott," he exclaimed. "If I had not lost mine half-crown, I would have had 12/6."

Wednesday Nov.11	This evening Liz went out and left the baby in her cradle. I made up my mind to have my face washed before lifting her. The baby made up her mind I wouldn't. I was determined and started my ablution. However, to be short, the baby won, and with my face half washed and my temper more than half lost, I had to lift her. Needless to say, I thought her an angel. In the evening I went to Mrs. Cockburn's, then bookkeeping class.
Thursday Nov. 12	Today an old man scarcely able to walk, holding his side with one hand and leaning on his stick with the other came into our back green and sang a song, *The Soldier's Tears*. Poor old soul! What a termination to a life! This is a great place for singers. One lately came and started *There is Beauty All Around*. I looked all round our back yard—I called it a green but it is innocent of grass. You might as well look for feathers on a dog as grass on our back "green". I felt much inclined to repudiate his statement. I wonder if it is my benevolent features that attract those sad singers?
Friday Nov. 13	I intended doing such a lot this evening. What I actually did was nothing at all. I held the baby a while then went with Liz to see Mrs Forbes who was ill.

Saturday Nov. 14	Today when coming along Princes Street with our lorry, I met Ned and Hughie Gollogly; they called me and told me that Mary, Hugh's wife, was dead. She was well in the forenoon and washed her floor at 12 o'clock. Early in the evening, she gave birth to a little daughter and everything seemed all right. When she suddenly became very ill and passed peacefully away. How very sad! How very uncertain is life. How little separates us from the grave. There is that fond mother taken away from her dear children at the very time they need her most. Yet there must be some purpose behind it all which we poor mortals cannot see. I grieve for poor Hugh. Mary requires no one's sympathy. I hope her soul is enjoying sweet repose.

In the afternoon I attended a jumble sale in Grindlay Street. I bought a lot of books. In the evening I attended a *Town Crier* meeting. It broke up about 11:20 p.m. Then I went up to Hughie's house for about half an hour. There I saw the last mortal remains of poor Mrs. Hugh Gollogly. What a contrast from when I saw you in your bridal beauty. And yet, Mary, you are beautiful in death.

Sunday Nov. 15	Today I attended the funeral of Hugh's wife. I was just thinking over it and between good health and her burial there were not fifty hours. Truly a very brief space. How mighty is the Hand of God. How very cruel seem Thy actions, oh Lord. Yet all Thy works are mixed with mercy and we will ever trust in Thee.

In the afternoon I went to Mr. Ross's church and heard a lecture on Blatchford v Ballard. After tea we went up to Mrs. Forbes'. She was ill.

Monday Nov. 16	In the evening, I went down to Mrs. Cockburn's. She is preparing quietly for a journey. What a terrible thing it must be for a couple to part in this manner after living together twenty-four years. I afterwards went to G.'s where I saw the poor little motherless baby whose birth had cost the mother her life. What a serious thing is life. One long continual worry. And looking round us we see people in greater worry and trouble and we have scarcely time to sympathise with them because of our own trials.

Trials and worry, worry and strife,
Losing life daily to keep in life.
Living in meagreness humblest of fare
Of the good things of life the poor get small share. |
Tuesday Nov. 17	This evening I had Mr. Cairns along. We had a most enjoyable evening with a talk over books, etc. I read over my essay on Wm. Cobbett to him and he praised it very much. It is to be read at our Guild. There will be—despite its many weaknesses—the usual flow of flattery. "I have listened with much pleasure to the excellent essay," which I believe in their inmost hearts they often know to be anything but excellent. I went home with Mr. Cairns and was back again at 11:20 p.m.
Wednesday Nov. 18	I did not feel like going out to face the elements tonight but wisely decided to go as I have a bookkeeping class on Wednesdays. How many a good project is lost forever in this manner. "Oh, I won't bother tonight," and as they won't bother any other night either, the good thing goes to the wall. Owing to this, I am myself in my present humble condition. I was home about 9:20 p.m.
Thursday Nov. 26	Guild in the evening. There was a symposium *Literary Edinburgh in the 18th Century*. There were some good stories told. One was: Hume, the historian, was returning home one night much the worse for liquor. He managed to stumble into a ditch where he lay crying for help for two hours. An old woman came along. "Are you Hume the atheist?" "Madam, I appeal to you in the name of Christian charity to help me out of this." "Charity or no charity, I'll no help ye oot o' there until you say the Creed and the Lord's Prayer." And he had to say them!

Friday Nov. 27	In the evening I went along to Mr. Hadden's for about an hour. Speaking on writing capabilities he said I could beat him at prose. I am, he said, better at prose than verse. And now I walk the street with all the airs of a literary man because Hadden says I can write prose. I am a fool but then, there are so many fools about that one needs to be an extra special fool to be noticed.
Saturday Nov. 28	It was raining when I went out this morning and it rained all day. Teenie's brother came here on a visit to Teen for a day. In the afternoon, he and I went into Cooke's Circus. It was very good. We had talks over various things later, when I found him to be very intelligent. He, however, does not approve of socialism. Nor does he approve of the state taking over the coal pits. He prefers to remain a wage slave to a money-grabbing company. He left about 8 o'clock. He is a good lad and we hope to see him back again soon.
Sunday Nov. 29	I intended doing a great deal today. My day's work summed up brings me to the conclusion that all I have done was nurse the baby. In the afternoon I went to McDermott's with baby. This is a splendid day. The air being bracing with a touch of frost. Yesterday, it rained from early morn till late at night. The weather is like men—it varies very much.

A company of soldiers sat down to dinner. "Any complaints?" asked the officer after the meal. "Yes, Sir," a recruit replied, "the praties are bad." "The what?" asked the officer. "Excuse that man, Sir," answered another full private. "He's ignorant. He means spuds."

Monday Nov. 30	On November 12th I took my first active part in the Guild, seconding a debate. The result was disastrous, the principal and I being the only voters on our side while there were ten on the other side. This evening I went up to 50 South Bridge and got five bills for the *Town Crier* which I distributed in the various newsagents. What a thankless task it is working on behalf of the working classes. This little monthly Labour paper is struggling for an existence, and the people spurning it are those it was started to help, the working classes. I remember seeing Queen, the editor, trying to sell a copy to a would-be swell on Calton Hill one Sunday evening. He refused, as one above such a paper. Yet he is a sweated brewery employee with hands on him like 'baps'.
Tuesday Dec. 1	We are now on the first day of the last month of the year. I remember when I used to look forward to the New Year coming, but now I never feel it coming. Soon another year will have slipped past and with it, another year of our existence. This evening, Robertson and I went round Stockbridge with *Town Crier*. We sold five and a half dozen to the various newsagents. I got home after 10 p.m. fairly tired out. I might have spent the evening more profitably at home by studying my bookkeeping, but study is not in my line. I believe I have a good brain but like the rest of my body it does not like to be harassed.
Wednesday Dec. 2	Wednesday is my bookkeeping class night. After falling asleep in a chair by the fireside, I awoke and wondered if I should go to the class or not. My better nature overcame my laziness and I went. What a beautiful mystery bookkeeping is to me. To make it worse, our teacher, a very able fellow, gets away so rapidly that I believe not one of his pupils can keep up with him.
Thursday Dec. 3	Mrs. Cockburn's in evening. After that I went to Guild where there was a Parliamentary Election between a Tory and a Liberal. The latter won by 8-3. In the after-business, Mr. Cairns asked me if I would act as critic on his essay "Charles Lamb". I consented though I have not the least knowledge of Lamb. That was rather stupid of me and quite up to my daily actions. Home with Mr. Cairns and home myself at 11:15 p.m.

Friday Dec. 4	Wm. Cobbett said one should write a little every day. That is good advice but I am quite at a loss what to write. I read the essay on "Charles Lamb" today and wrote out a little of my criticism on it. In the evening, I went in for Ned and we went to the "Sons" meeting together. This was the shortest meeting I have attended with the Sons.
Saturday Dec. 5	In the usual manner, I wasted this afternoon and to waste the rest of my evening Liz and I and baby went visiting. We enjoyed ourselves but of course, it was so much more time wasted. I am what could be called a "waster". Some time ago, there appeared in our minutes in the "Sons" book a bit of very disagreeable business that seemed like getting another into an awkward fix. To get him out of it, the blame was rolled out to me as a mistake on my part. It was rough on me to soothe matters a bit but I stood it.
Sunday Dec. 6	Up early this morning and after the usual slashing at tea I wrote out my criticism on Mr. Cairn's essay. I then went on with the remainder of my own essay and finished the first volume of Smith's Biography of Cobbett. What a wonderful man Cobbett was to be sure, and yet he is practically unknown at the present day.
Monday Dec. 7	Home early in the afternoon. There was a young man in our backyard today singing, a strong able-looking young man. I wonder was he genuinely in want or did he deserve help. What a gang of rogues beggars are. I heard of one who got two slices of bread and butter given him and when he got down the stair he stuck them with the butter against the back of the stair door. Another one pretending to be lame was offered bread by an old Irish woman. "Couldn't you give me a copper instead?" and he used a nasty word which got the Irish woman's blood up and she made for him. The manner in which he sprinted away showed that he was anything but lame.

Tuesday Dec. 8	What a lot of busy people are going about just now saying the cause of Britain's failure to compete with other countries is the "ca-canny" system. What a lot of work they do going about airing out blether, and telling the poor working man, whose hands are horny, whose face is worn and haggard, and whose back is bent with toil, that he does not work hard enough. The mischief is that lots of working men believe it. Such a thing as the exhorbitant profits to the capitalist will never dawn on them. This evening I went over and interviewed the Canadian Agent with a view to going to that great colony. The conditions—10/ weekly and board—did not suit me. The land may be flowing with milk and honey but it is meal and cold water for the poor labourers. What a crime it is to be poor.
Wednesday Dec. 9	This evening I intended going to Mrs Cockburn's and then to the class. I got comfortably sat down in Mrs C.'s and learning could go to the dogs. This is how the working class is so far behind in education. They simply won't take the bother to learn.
Thursday Dec. 10	This evening I went up to Mr. Cairns and accompanied him to the Guild. He read his essay on Charles Lamb and I acted as critic. I made but a poor job of reading my paper. I can't control my nerves some way or other, besides I had been altering it here and there and that mixed me a little. Mr. Cairns, however, told me that I did splendidly.
Friday Dec. 11	I have not sent anything in for next month's *Town Crier*. I am going off poetry now. I expect poets have their seasons and I am simply off-season. Our baby is very ill tonight. She is fevered and fretting. This makes a great difference as she is usually very much the other way. Her teeth are the cause of the trouble. She was bright and smiling this morning. What a change a few hours bring about. How I wish I saw all this suffering past and baby with all her teeth. It is a pity that nature—hard-hearted old dame—could not see her way clear to give children teeth without taking payment in children suffering.

Saturday Dec. 12	In the afternoon, Tom, Jock Imrie and I attended Lord Rosebery's Free Trade meeting in the Synod Hall. Like myself, I believe lots of others went more to see the man than to hear Free Trade "gush". In the evening, I went up to the library. In the afternoon I was in seeing Tom's mother, a true stamp of an old Irish woman, full of wit and folk lore and rheumatics. I had a few good stories from her. She is very superstitious.
Sunday Dec. 13	Spent the greater part of today reading up on Cobbett. Did not get on very well with my essay. In the afternoon, I went to class when Miss R. waxed eloquent on the Commandments. In the evening, Liz and I went to Forbes'.
Monday Dec. 14	Went to Guild Council meeting, 22 Queen St., where I heard a discussion on "Some Modern Foes of Religion". It was very interesting and I enjoyed the meeting very much. I got home at 11:20 p.m. The leading speaker there, I noticed could not keep himself still while he was sitting but would continually 'touch up' his moustache, or stroke his small beard. I believe he did it unconsciously but the habit arises out of conceit.
Tuesday Dec. 15	Mrs Cockburn's in the evening with Liz. I went up to the library for Mrs C.
Wednesday Dec. 16	For a long time past a young couple living up our stair have been anxious to speak to us. The other day, the young woman, Mrs. Nicol, did so, and my wife invited her down to our house for tea. This afternoon, while she was sitting in our house, she got a postcard about their returning to Hawick—their native place—so that is a close of friendship severed ere friendship formed. At 7:30 p.m. I went to Mrs. Robertson's, St. David's Terrace. Then class at 8 p.m.

Thursday Dec. 17	I have just heard a story. It comes from America and is American, pure and simple. A little child, aged three months, while being washed by its mother, turned round and said, "Mother, at this time next year you will have a sore ear." The mother was thunderstruck and went for a neighbour who was in the habit of coming in and speaking to the child. She took up the child and said, "Did you say your mother would have a sore ear next year?" "Yes," the child answered distinctly and fell back in the woman's arms dead. I have heard many an American yarn, but that one simply takes the biscuit factory.
Friday Dec. 18	I intended being out early tonight but the usual hindrance came in the way—the baby. A baby is all right so long as it is quiet but you will find that if you want a quiet moment, the baby will be quiet until just then—and look out for squalls. I had such a lot to do, and as usual just got through half of it with a rush, visiting Robertson, High Riggs, the library and then the "Son's" meeting. Came home in company with Ned Gollogly who waxed eloquent on religion.
Saturday Dec. 19	I have just heard that my American story of two days ago is a Welsh story and did not relate to its mother's ear but to next year. The people all round believe the story and are looking forward to a bad year. This is the first Saturday I can remember for a long time that I have not been out in the afternoon or evening. I have a bad cold. This afternoon we cleaned our house. I papered our small lobby. Our baby was crying fit to break her heart while lying in her cradle a minute ago. Immediately on being lifted she changed her tune. It is very aggravating but one displays a great weakness by losing one's temper on such occasions.

Sunday Dec. 20	I have lately made some successful attempts at controlling my temper. On Friday evening, Liz was giving me a lengthy lecture for going out at nights. She was as angry as she was eloquent. "Liz, my dear, if ever I take another wife I'll see that she is a dumby." This made her laugh and finished the lecture for the time being . Later, when paying my cards at the "Son's" I was asked for tickets I should have had with me. I remarked that I had forgotten them. "Next," said he, and went on with the other books, leaving me until the last . I said very little but felt like saying a lot. I **was** angry. Today I had a go at my essay. Wrote to Maud Robin and visited Forbes' afternoon and evening. They are preparing to go to Canada. In them we lose very dear friends.

Monday Dec. 21	Some people are unable to distinguish between impudence and cleverness. Some time ago, Liz and I were in company where there was a little boy who kept on imitating Lizzie's talk in a most aggravating manner, much to the delight of his parents who said he was always clever. Were he my child he would not be so "clever". He would have less cleverness and be the better of it.

Got p.c. to attend *Town Crier* meeting but did not attend owing to a cold.

Tuesday Dec. 22	Some years ago I was talking to a woman about the different traits in her family. How very careful she was to put down all their good points to her side. This is a natural failing and is to be found in men also.

Tonight we went down to Mrs. Cockburn's and paid her two pounds for machine. She is in a terrible state. Liz says she does not think Mrs. C. will live long now. I shall be sorry to lose her friendship.

> But the hand of God bids us to sever.
> God put us not on earth forever.
> Think when we miss a loving heart
> That the very 'best of friends must part.'

Tollcross looking towards High Riggs and Lauriston Place, c. 1900.

Wednesday Dec. 23	There is a saying that between the bride and the bridegroom the former is the cheapest as she is "given away", when the bridegroom is generally "sold". My idea of a lot of marriages is that instead of being sold, the bridegroom is more often "thrown away".

This afternoon with the aid of our lorry, I brought home our machine from C.'s. For a whole week I have not opened my bookkeeping book. They say that "practice makes perfect". Then for want of practice, I shall never be perfect. |
| Thursday
Dec. 24 | This morning I got a nice letter and Christmas card from Stephenson. His letter brought sad news of death and was sadly blotted at the part telling us of it. This showed how my dear friend must have felt the loss. This is Christmas Eve and we are told to be merry. What mockery! "Let all men rejoice." Think of these words as you look into the unshaved and starving faces of our unemployed. Think of their wives and if you are not moved to tears, think of their children. How inadequate do I feel myself to write my thoughts. God help those people! For left to the mercy of men they fare but poorly. "Peace on Earth, Goodwill to all men." |
| Friday
Dec. 25 | This is Christmas day. We had nice Christmas cards from Ned and Maggie and from Teen's brother. I sent cards to no person but I wish everybody a very Merry Christmas. How I would that I could make it merrier and happier for some of them. In the evening I visited Gollogly's for a short time. Then went to Queen's and went out with *Town Crier*s. Robertson and I disposed of fifteen dozen. I went to McDermotts later. Thus ended my Christmas day. |

Saturday Dec. 26	Today I went up to Queen's. He was highly elated over the success of sending out the boys with *Town Criers*. For nine months he has worked very hard with this little paper for the sum of nothing a year payable in advance. I was home at 6:30 p.m. and went out with Liz shopping. Home and in bed at 10 p.m.
	"Early to bed, early to rise, makes a man healthy, wealthy and wise." I learned that old saw when I was very young but have never yet seen much wisdom in it. I have been an early bedder and early riser all my life. I believe I am healthy, I think I am wise, but wealthy I am not.
Sunday Dec. 27	Wrote to Mr. and Mrs. Cook then took baby out for an hour (Handy man!). After dinner, Ned, Maggie and Jim G. were along. There were nine of us sat down to tea. I have missed a few Sundays at our class this session. For the past four sessions I was pretty regular but lately I have fallen off. So much for being married. We are now in the last week of the year.
Monday Dec. 28	Some months ago I undertook to write an essay on Wm. Cobbett. All these months I let slip past and I am now on the last four days and have to make a sprint. I used up this entire evening writing it—or part of it. Here is a Cobbett story on courtship: A young man on a visit to his sweetheart's, heard her asking her sisters, "Where is our needle?" Now the fact that they had only one needle and did not know where that needle was, proved too much for him and he made himself scarce.
Tuesday Dec. 29	Again spent the evening with Cobbett. Another Cobbett story: this time on marriage. "When my wife was confined in Philadelphia she could not go to sleep owing to the barking of dogs outside. I went outside and kept running about 200 yards each side of our house throwing stones at those dogs. This I did all night. When I came in, got myself dressed and went out to a day's business that was to keep me till six o'clock. If my wife had not got sleep on that occasion, she would have died." This is a case of a man going to the dogs.

Wednesday Dec. 30	This is Mr. and Mrs. Forbes' 22nd Anniversary of their marriage. Liz and I were up there and spent the evening. Very enjoyable. They are an ideal couple and I am ever doing my best to copy him. I have a good wife and any little attention I pay her is not wasted.
Thursday Dec. 31	This is Hogmanay Day. In the evening I went with Liz to her dressmaker's. Then my Aunt Lizzie. My mother came up and gave our baby a nice toy cat. As the New Year came in we went up, Liz and I, to Mr. and Mrs. Nicol's up the stair and were their first-foot. They then came down to our house and were ours. Annie and her man also came in and after some fun they dispersed and we went to bed at 3:30 a.m.. The people all round us are 'enjoying' themselves and are all very drunk. I wonder how they appreciate such muddled happiness. Such happiness, too, often ends in injured good looks, the result of fighting.

REFLECTIONS ON 1903

This is the first full year of our married life. It has been happy indeed! We have lost through death many friends. Early in the year, Mrs. Innes, dear old soul! Then Gilby and others. Our baby was born in May and has thrived well up to date. A new Labour paper has been started in Edinburgh with which I have become connected. It has struggled on well and is now in its ninth month. We removed to a bigger house—our first one was £4.12.0. Our second is £7.0.0 yearly.

I have been closer connected with our Guild and have this year taken a prominent part in a debate on Municipal Trading: criticised an essay on Charles Lamb by Mr. Cairns: written some poetry on the departure of ex-President L. Dalgleish who went to South Africa; and written an essay on William Cobbett.

I am a delegate to the Church Council and member of Committee.

1904
Friday
Jan. 1

The old year has gone and is now as far away as any past year. But many of its affairs are still with us. And so it is, the years blend one with another and make as it were branches on a great tree called TIME. In the forenoon, Liz, baby and I went to the Forbes'. In the afternoon we went to Aunt Lizzie's where we had tea. We returned at about 7:30 p.m. I was fagged out and went to bed. In the evening our baby was very cross and raised my ire very much. However, the loss of my temper didn't seem to concern baby much and I had just to find my temper again.

Saturday
Jan. 2

A snowy morning. I started work at 6:00 a.m. and finished at 10:00 a.m. In the afternoon I went to the funeral of an old friend, Wm. Primrose. On his deathbed he said, "I hope to God none of my family will lead a life like mine." What a text. He passed away, a done man at something like forty-four years. Just a few years ago he was as fine a specimen of manhood as you would wish to see, and with care his life might have been spared another fifty years. But he enjoyed it and made it short as a result. Poor Primrose! With all my heart I wish you may rest in peace. You were a good fellow, but weak when tempted.

Sunday
Jan. 3

Our baby is now getting on nicely and can stand by holding on to a chair. She is seven and a half months old. She is full of life and can hardly be put to sleep, springing and screaming often at 10:30 p.m.

Tonight Liz put her to bed and went out for a minute—I was in, of course. Imagine Lizzie's surprise to see baby sitting bolt upright in bed and taking notice of her as soon as she came in. It was funny to see her holding against her mother trying to make her lie down. And it was only after I had carried her up and down the floor for some time she did sleep. Had visit from Mr. and Mrs. Martin, Musselburgh, in afternoon. In evening, Liz and I visited Mrs. Cockburn.

Monday Jan. 4	I have been thinking today on an old man—an "unco guid"—who used to go to Church three times a Sunday and drag his unfortunate family along with him. Oh, spare me from a church-going father. Rather give me an atheist one. On any of his sons being unable to go, he would give them a good few verses from the Bible to learn off by heart by his return under pain of severe punishment. One would naturally think the sons would have turned out "unco guids", but no—and oh, how it grieves me to tell it—I once saw one of that family—a man now—drink on a Sunday. What a waste of energy on the old man's part. In the evening I was at Cockburn's and library. Mrs. C.'s last week here.
Tuesday Jan. 5	A few short years ago I was at a marriage where the bride and groom looked tall and handsome and strong. The life and soul of the company was also big and strong, Wm. Primrose. The bride and Primrose are now gone to their last accounts and the groom now broods and looks into the fire and spits, a done man. What a change death makes and there is nothing we are so sure of. In the afternoon I went up to Mr. McKenzie's re Mrs. C.'s furniture. He came down with me in the evening and bought them.
Wednesday Jan. 6	Today I saw the military funeral of a Mr. Fraser, from 80 Temple Park Crescent. He was one of the last of the "Thin Red Line". The Pipe band of the R. H. played slowly along Temple Park. On gaining Yeoman Pl. they stopped playing and went off into a quick march and a poor old soul among the mourners who was being supported by two young men had to drop out. He must have felt to fall out of the cortege. This was a genuine respect [but] what was the soldiers'? They make a splended show but it ends there. Respect is a thing unknown to them. Mrs. C.'s in evening. A wild night after a stormy day.

Thursday Jan. 7	This is an important evening, as I have to read my essay on William Cobbett this evening. Eight years ago I used to envy the abilities of the various members as they read their papers. Had I remained a member, no doubt I would have had a paper long before now. We had Aunt Lizzie and Cousin Bella along to tea. A van came in the evening with some things I had bought.
Friday Jan. 8	Thank Goodness! My essay is finished and read. There was a good attendance of the Guild last night and my essay had a most favourable reception. One member said it was the best-written essay he had heard for a long time. Others spoke in a like manner. Of course, there has to be some allowance made for superfluous flattery.
Saturday Jan. 9	This afternoon we were all in a laughable and enjoyable mood at our house. Liz and I got ready to go to the Carnival in the Waverley Market and were actually on the way thither when she cast out with the manner in which I was dressed and left me in Dalry Road. I went on with baby and had an enjoyable afternoon visiting my friends. In the evening, Liz and I visited Mrs. Cockburn. It was a very cold night.
Sunday Jan. 10	There are times when I feel as if I could write on for a long time and times when I cannot write a bit. The present is one of the latter times. Our baby is getting on very well and has now two teeth. Sometimes Liz wishes she had no teeth. These times are when she bites her breast in sucking. This is a miserable day of rain and snow. I visited Hadden in the morning and wrote to Stephenson later.
Monday Jan. 11	What a great thing is fate. Some men are great because they are simply pitchforked into it. While others with greater minds remain in obscurity. Tonight I visited Mrs. Cockburn's. She was gone and Mr. Cockburn had just discovered that some of the furniture had been sold. He told me the whole story carefully omitting his own faults. Liz and I went down to the station to see Mrs. C off. However, we never saw her. She must have gone with an earlier train. It was keen frost and we could hardly walk home. Home at 12:10 a.m.

Tuesday Jan. 12	Tonight I hunted high and low, all over our house for my bookkeeping books. Liz also searched but in vain. I think we looked too well and believe some time when we are not wanting nor looking for them we will find them. In fact, they'll be lying in our road somewhere. Last night, I gave Hadden a small piece of my poetry to criticise. I called in later expecting to see my verses all red-marked with alterations. Judge my surprise to find that he approved of it as it was. I must be becoming a great 'Poet'. Excuse the capital "P". Tonight Liz and I visited the Waxwork. It was very quiet and, excepting some very famous persons in wax, we were the only ones present. Today I saw a poor lame woman singing in Caley Cres. She had two small boys hanging on to her skirt and a baby in her arms. "Ye Banks and Braes" was her song. I was struck with the part: "How can ye sing, ye little birds, and I sae weary—fu' o' care." Now the first part of that statement I could have challenged at once, as there was not a bird singing for miles around, but the latter part—poor soul—never were there words said with more seeming truth for wearied and fu' o' care she certainly looked.
Wednesday Jan. 13	Another search for bookkeeping books. Again in vain. I did not go to the class. Visited Aunt Lizzie. This afternoon we had a visit from Miss Robertson who gave me a small book in a present. For five years this lady has given us a present every year. She has displayed great taste in her choice. Each of the little books have been, of course, of a religious nature.
Thursday Jan. 14	Last session at our Guild. Business meeting. I was appointed Delegate to the Fellowship Section to the Church Council. Last year our delegates were called THE INVISIBLE MEN owing to their never being seen at the meetings. I have missed the first two or three meetings but attended tonight. There was a good attendance and a paper was read on "How to Manage a Sunday School", to be followed by a discussion. I did not wait to hear the discussion.

47

Friday Jan. 15	Some time ago I started this diary with the intention of writing a page every day. To show you how I hold to my intentions, there is sometimes a fortnight passes and I don't see the book. Then I am busy writing up arrears, a little for each lost day. The task as I intended should only occupy a minute or two each day but when it falls back, it takes me over half an hour, which is practically lost time. Sons of Temperance meeting in the evening. This makes six months I have been in office in that Society.
Saturday Jan. 16	Some years ago a lady visited the house of a poor woman who was going to throw out a stale half-loaf. She asked the lady if she would take it to her hens. She took the bread, and on going back the poor woman asked her did her hens eat the bread. "No," she replied. "I ate it myself." She thus gave the woman a much-needed lesson in economy. In the evening, Liz and I went to the shows where she met some people she knew.
Sunday Jan. 17	On Saturday nights I generally make up my mind to rise early on the Sunday morning. This morning I held to that much abused intention by getting up at 8:45 a.m. Instead of 7 a.m. as intended. In the afternoon Mr. and Mrs Nicol were down to tea. Later we all went down to McDermott's where we all had another slash of tea. This is a custom. It is supposed friendliness to give visitors tea. It is a bad form and the worst of it is that it is unfriendly to refuse.
Monday Jan. 18	Yesterday I made Mr. Nicol make up his mind to join the "Sons". What a mistake it is for a man not to be in a society. "Oh, I won't bother just now," they say—as if it was bother. It is rather to save bother it should be done. Tonight I visited Tom and then went to "Gardeners'" Annual Meeting.

Tuesday Jan. 19	Tonight our Guild has an inter-debate on with Currie Parish Church. I intended going but got a p.c. today from "Son's" secretary to come to his house this evening. Rich men have their hobbies, so have poor men. I don't know the hobbies of the various rich men, but I know that mine is books. Like many another poor man with a hobby, I cannot go very far with it. This evening I visited "Son's" secretary and got ten shillings salary for acting as Recording Secretary for six months. I would fain have spent it on my hobby, there being some nice book stalls on my way.
Wednesday Jan. 20	My bookkeeping night. The most essential part of learning is practice. I ought to practise bookkeeping but like many another thing I should do, I simply don't; with the result that I am, as far as bookkeeping is concerned, a duffer. I am not the worst in our class, there being several other duffers there. A splendid way to sharpening a blunt intellect is a steady application to practice.
Thursday Jan. 21	Tonight I did not go out. I got a book from the library *How to Speak Extempore*. Had it been "how to sleep extempore" I had mastered it ere I was half through with it as I fell asleep reading it. I slipped ben the room and lay down on the sofa where I slept for an hour. Liz came in search of me, to give me a job, I expect, but did not see me on the sofa and I escaped.
Friday Jan. 22	In the evening, Tom McD. and I went to our Guild's Burns' Concert. There was a silver collection. In the plate there was a goodly amount of pennies and thirteen half-pence. They looked rather out of place in a silver collection. What a blessing it is for lots of people that Burns lived. Lots of them live or add to their incomes through the enthusiasm raised annually by his anniversary. Ours was a splendid concert and much enjoyed.

Saturday Jan. 23	This afternoon Liz is in the huff. It is a misunderstanding of a suggestion of mine that has offended her. I remember I used to be much concerned on occasions like this; but now it would take a double strong microscope to discover a riffle on my countenance. Tonight McD., Robertson, Hadden and I went to meeting of *Crier* contributors where we spent a good time discussing the paper. I got home at 11:30 p.m. and found Liz in bed with toothache and dumps. I don't know which was hurting her most.
Sunday Jan. 24	This morning I was up first. 7:30 a.m. I made the breakfast and did some writing and otherwise wasted the evening. I went to class at 5 p.m. in afternoon. I arranged with Miss R. for an hour's bookkeeping on Mondays from 6 to 7 p.m. I visited Mrs. Robertson's, St. David's Terrace, later. She was in trouble over her son leaving his work. When I came home, Liz was out, grieved at me for being so late.
Monday Jan. 25	This is Burns's Birthday. On this day something over 100 years ago the world was presented with one of the greatest geniuses ever born. His was a life of comedy and tragedy. It would be difficult to write something new about that truly great man. This evening I went up to Miss R.'s and had a profitable hour at arithmetic. I came home and had a further lesson.
Tuesday Jan. 26	I went with Liz this evening up to Napier's, the Herbalist. After that I went to a Store concert in Oddfellows Hall. The best part of it was the soiree by Mr. Mallance. Instead of giving us some remarks, tortured us with a speech lasting over half an hour. Speaking of Provident Societies he said, "We must keep the wolf away from the door." Just then there was a rustling and rattling at the door and I was hoping it would get in and come right up and devour the Chairman.

| Wednesday | A well-known D.D., a preacher to the late Queen, too— |
| Jan. 27 | was once in a middle of an eloquent discourse when the stillness was broken by a baby crying. The mother rose to go out. "Don't go away, my good woman, baby is not disturbing me." "No, but you're disturbing baby," came the unexpected reply. Tonight I went to the bookkeeping class, and again showed how little I know about the subject. |

| Thursday | Tonight I went up for Mr. Cairns and went with him to |
| Jan. 28 | our Guild where we had a splendid essay on Goldsmith. What a wonderful mortal was Goldsmith. I have heard that if he were returning home with some money he had borrowed and a beggar accosted him, he would think nothing of giving the beggar all his money. Thus he was always a beggar himself. A friend of ours has a baby boy who is always crying. He puts me in mind of the heir to the British throne. The Prince of Wails, you know. |

| Friday | Tonight I took Nichol to pass Dr. and join the Sons of |
| Jan. 29 | Temperance. This is the half-yearly meeting and it was rather a tedious job taking the minutes. This evening I went to Store and left my measure for a new suit. This is such an unusual event that I take note of it. It is nearly three years since I got a new suit. A police court is a strange place to think that there are as many lawyers, police and others and there are suits lost there every day. |

| Saturday | This afternoon, instead of going round with the *Crier*, I |
| Jan. 30 | went with Liz to Store where she bought a new jacket for herself. This is also a rare occurrence. In the evening, Liz, Annie, Teen and I went to the Carters' Concert in Oddfellows Hall. The chairman addressing some rowdies said, "I will advise you carters not to descend to the level of University students." The remark had the desired effect. |

| Sunday | Got up early this morning. Held baby awhile, then wrote |
| Jan. 31 | minutes of "Son's" meeting. Read part of *The Vicar of Wakefield* during the day. Class at 5 p.m. Home at 6:10 p.m. Liz. was at Forbes' and came from there in a dreadful temper. Got on to me in an awful manner because I didn't go up to take her out. However, it finished up in the usual manner and we were friends this evening. |

Monday Feb. 1	It is often the case that while we are engaged remembering some petty thing or other, we forget something of more importance. This evening I wasted my time over trifles when I should have been at Miss R.'s at 6 o'clock. I arrived at 6:40 p.m. Home at 8:10 p.m. Of all the things I find difficulty in learning arithmetic and bookkeeping are the hardest to me. I simply get lost in figures.
Tuesday Feb. 2	February has started badly. Yesterday morning when I went out I was surprised to see a dirty, wet morning. The night before was splendid. It has rained continually since. We who are carrying coal in dirty, wet bags are having rather a bad time.
Wednesday Feb. 3	Still dirty weather. How comfortable everybody is. We are all prospering and happy and yet we are slaving and working in a place that a pig would think twice and not go into. The people who talk about the wealth and welfare of the nation are generally those that have a very big share of it. This evening Tom and I went around with *Criers*.
Thursday Feb. 4	This evening I went to Store and got new suit fitted on. Liz and I then went up to see the Fire Brigade turn out as there is a false alarm on. We didn't wait long enough to see it. I went to the Guild later. It is magazine night. I had three pieces in: "Oh, Daddy Will I See the King": "To Leslie B. Dalgliesh", and a letter on the Burns' concert. Home early as baby is not so well this evening. She is cutting her teeth, and as teeth are a possession very much envied, she is having to pay for them.
Friday Feb. 5	Tonight I went up to *Crier* office and got some bills, then came along and went into Ned's for half an hour. Later I took William Sloan and William Grant out to become members of the "Gardeners'". Maggie bad with her teething tonight. She was very fidgety and could not be pacified. When I took her she was quiet at once. Before putting her into bed I had to walk up and down the floor and sing about 200 songs to her.

52

Saturday Feb. 6	This afternoon, Annie, Liz and I went to the Store sale where the ladies bought goods. In the evening, we went to Waverley Market where, with wet feet and ear unenraptured, I listened to a musical concert given by the Black Watch. It rained heavily, as it has done all week.
Sunday Feb. 7	Up early this morning. As usual made a poor use of the day. In the afternoon out with wee Mag. to McD.'s, then class at 5 p.m. At 6:30 p.m., I went to St. Cuthbert's U.F. Church Hall and heard a splendid discourse on the evils of drink. One example was; A man went to an hospital where the Dr. told him that he took drink. "Yes," replied the patient. "I have taken it all my life but it has never done me any harm." "Well," said the surgeon, "I am not in the habit of standing tipple, but for the sake of experiment, I will stand you one." "Right," replied the patient. The whisky was soon forthcoming. Now previous to taking the drink he made him read a paper from as far back as he could read. After taking the dram, he tried again at the same mark but could not see the print. He had to come forward a few paces to see it.

As a schoolmaster, he has seen some strange sights. A very common one was: A boy fainted in the school. He was taken outside and given some bread and milk and quickly came round. It was starvation was the cause of the fainting.

After the meeting had a walk with Liz and baby. She is very cross owing to her teeth.

Monday Feb. 8	For some time past, Japan and Russia have been at variance. Today started war between them. Last night the Japanese sent in three torpedoes to Port Arthur and damaged three of Russia's best ships. What a terrible thing war is to be sure. Wellington said that the worst thing next to a battle won is a battle lost. So that war, winning or losing is terrible indeed.

Tuesday Feb. 9	All is excitement over the Eastern war. The Fiscal Policy is simply in the background. What a mixed affair is the human mind. Always looking out for something sensational and being carried away with important things far away from him and forgetting important things nearer home. Today the Japanese damaged another four Russian warships. This is splendid for both Japan and the newspaper press.
Wednesday Feb. 10	This is my bookkeeping class night but as I have fallen too far back in the race, I drop out. I am a duffer at many things but at figures I am something even worse.
Thursday Feb. 11	Went a short walk with Liz and baby after which I went to Guild and heard the reading of an essay on Goldsmith by Mr. Cairns.
Friday Feb. 12	This was the first meeting of the half yr. of the "Sons". I was there and read the minutes of the last half year meeting.
Saturday Feb. 13	For the first time for many months, I went to see a football match—Celtic v. St. Bernard's Scottish Cup Tie. Result: Celtic 4—Saints 0. There was a very heavy downpour of rain and the spectators flocked from the ground. Some of the players likely wished they could do likewise. In the evening I took the Chair at the Clinton Cricket Club Annual meeting. We had a lively time. Today a poor women was singing in Fountainbridge. She had three children. The police motioned from the other side for her to shift. I saw her face contracting and the tears coming. And yet we are a rich nation. How ill-divided our riches are.
Sunday Feb. 14	Another rainy day. I did not go out until the evening when I went along to Robertson's, High Riggs, and met Liz coming from the Mission meeting.
Monday Feb. 15	For some time past I have been out nearly every night and as constant dripping will wear away a stone, and my wife's patience does not last nearly as long as a stone, my going out caused some domestic friction. She now declares my staying indoors as a nice change.

Saturday Feb. 27	The long intervals frequently met with in this book—the spaces between the dates show them—will show you how diligent I am with my "daily" diary. In the course of a day there are many things come into my mind which I intend entering in my diary at night. Like many others of my projects, it nearly always falls through. Today I was out with *Criers* in afternoon and evening. Visited Robertson, High Riggs, in evening. Baby keeping well and now on the mention of "clap handie" she immediately does so. She also says, "ta-ta" very distinctly. She is getting on very well and is the source of my joy in our home.
Sunday Feb. 28	Yesterday I got home a new suit from the Store. It cost £2.12.6. Today I had it on for the first time. It is a splendid fit. Some men have a different suit for every day, but with me it is a novelty. I went to class in afternoon. During the day I visited a number of friends.
Monday Feb. 29	This is the first Feb. 29th for eight years. Now this is rough on girls who were born on Feb. 29th and look forward to that date for presents. Of course I know there are very few girls look for presents. In fact, they'll hardly take one. In the evening I went up to Miss R.'s and had one and a half hours arithmetic. This has been a severe month. It came in like a lion; became like a den of lions and went out like a menagerie.
Tuesday March 1	March has come in like a lion—a snow-white lion. It is very uncomfortable walking against a snowstorm and not likely to mend a broken temper. This evening, I intended going out to the gymnastic class but did not get much nearer it than my own fireside. Lydia left her place today at 9:00 a.m. and took the 10:15 a.m. for Cardiff.
Wednesday March 2	Today there was a woman begging in a stair I was up. She was a big, sturdy-looking woman. I expect she went to every door in the stair without receiving anything. She stood at the foot of the stair awhile and I saw the tears coming from her eyes. Woman's inhumanity to woman made that woman mourn. And yet we wonder why our race is degenerating and this big sturdy woman cannot get a bite of food in this rich country. In the evening I was out house-hunting with Liz.

Thursday March 3	I remember a good many years ago—perhaps fourteen years when, I would be about fourteen years of age. A friend and I went hunting all over the town for rubber with which to make catapults. After an unsuccessful evening and we were home again to Freer Street, it struck me we might try a little shop at the head of the street. We did and we got what we wanted there. Then we got outside and were near kicking ourselves. In the evening I went to Guild with books then came away and had a walk with Jim and Ned. Wee Mag. was peevish today—probably her teeth is the cause of it.
Friday March 4	The driver on whose lorry I work at present—I will not spoil my diary with his name—is a man with whom I cannot become reconciled. This is owing to his close-mindedness with regard to our routes. He simply won't tell his fellow-workers where they are going to. For this and sundry other mean dodges he is universally disliked by the men. He won't put an extra piece in a worker's bag but just to show you the consistency of this double-dyed hypocrite, he will steal biscuits by the pound from the Society. A very honest man is—dash it all, I nearly put in his name. Honest enough but worth watching. I could fill my book with stories of his meanness and silliness, but like his name, they would only stain the book.
Saturday March 5	This afternoon, Teenie's brother and his wife-to-be were through here from a mining place near Glasgow. In the afternoon I went to the funeral of Tom Robertson's father, Hugh Robertson. He was hale and hearty on Monday and is buried today. How uncertain is life and how certain is death. Liz and I had walk round Town and then saw friends off at Waverley Station.
Sunday March 6	This afternoon Miss Robertson spoke to the class on the Taking of Jericho. The Israelites went in and destroyed man, woman and child at the point of the sword. "A unique victory," said Miss R. "A bloody cruel and callous massacre" is what I would call it. Coalman's Mission with Liz in evening, then Forbes' where baby was.

Monday March 7	Liz washing today. I should have gone to Miss R.'s for instruction on bookkeeping. Did not go out this evening. I intended reading a lot but instead of working my brain I rested it. Not being half an hour reading when I went to sleep. This is a drawback from which I have suffered all my life. At the most interesting of books I will go to sleep. Some years ago during an illness I could not sleep. I got up and started to read. That did it. I was asleep in a very short time. Sleepy head!
Tuesday March 8	Today I quarrelled with Liz. This has been averted through me controlling my temper. Today I gave way with results not to be envied. In the evening I went along to Ned's. Ned came with me to library. We afterwards visited the Reference Dept. of the library. It was a dirty, rainy night. Hugh G. is far from well. Dr. Robertson visited him lately. He said Hughie is done, but may last for years yet. About seven or eight years ago he was a strapping and strong a lad as you would have wished to see. But now—poor Hugh.
Wednesday March 9	Tonight when at the Empire with Ned, he told me the following joke: A 'veteran' from South Africa went into a barbers and in a surly tone said, "I want a shave. And, look here, if you give me the least scratch, I'll put a bullet through you." So saying, he laid a revolver on the table. The barber shaved him without a hitch. "You were very cool," said the soldier. "Oh, I was running no risk. If I had given you the least scratch I would have cut your head off."
Thursday March 10	Guild in evening. Hat night. Debates concerning Municipal Elections, Total Abstinence, and the Yellow Peril. After seeing Mr. Cairns home, I got home at 11:10 p.m.
Friday March 11	"Sons" in the evening. Debate on what salary to give the doctor for Cadets. In my opinion, he is a grabby mortal and will give nothing away.

E 57

Wednesday
March 16

For some time I have neglected my 'daily' diary. I am prompted to write today's by a very sad occurrence. Mrs. Gilbertson a very dear friend of mine has passed away this morning. God help her five bairns! As for her, she needs no help. She has now passed through the Land of the Shadow of Death and I believe enjoying that peace she so richly deserves. My sister, Annie, was taken badly too this afternoon and Liz is attending her and doing her housework. Baby is cross tonight. Her teeth are troubling her, I think. This morning, Mrs. McDermott gave birth to a daughter. It is a fine fat baby and its parents are more than proud of it. Early this morning in a fire at Duddingston a fireman was killed. He saw a great wall falling and tried to excape it, but was too late. What a terrible death. He saw it coming.

Thursday
March 17

Tonight I went along and viewed the remains of Mrs. Gilbertson. How well she looked. We never know when Death will lay his cold clammy hand on our shoulder and say, "You next!" and we cannot say, "Nay". I may live for fifty or sixty years yet; I may die tomorrow, but till my dying day I will never cease to respect Mrs. Gilbertson's memory. She was one of the most loving mothers and an ideal wife. God have mercy on her. While in Mrs Gilbertson's house this evening, I met Mrs McPhillips, Leith. We had a long talk in which she told me that her bairns—one of which, Wee Maggie, I stood godfather for about six years ago—are all getting on very well. I am glad to hear it and wish they may all get on well for a long time yet. Guild in evening when I heard a fine essay on Louis Stevenson by Mr. Wilson.

Friday
March 18

This evening Liz and I went along to Mrs. Gilbertson's where Liz saw that dear soul's remains for the last time. People say we should not regret death, it a happy change and all that. That may be so, but it is no happy change for her offspring. And I regret her death very much. Wee Mag. is getting on very well and will now kiss you when you ask her to.

| Saturday March 19 | I have just returned from Mrs. Gilbertson's funeral. The scene in the house was one of the most pathetic I have ever witnessed. Especially at the point when the children took the parting kiss at their dear, dear mother. Oh, that those cold clammy lips had been able to return those kisses. What a warmth would have been there. But alas! those lips are silent now and one of the warmest and most affectionate of hearts is still. Poor Ellen! The tears I have shed for you are genuine. I wonder if she is now with her Tom! What thoughts come into one's head. It just occurred to me that Tom had been beckoning to Ellen and she has answered his call. It may be silly, but I think it a nice thought that they are again united. A sort of Heavenly Wedding with angels as guests and God as Priest and the happy union to go on forever and ever. Amen!

Liz also came to funeral with baby in coach. Baby was very cross and had to be carried all the way back. Complaint? Dental. |
|---|---|
| Sunday March 20 | Ellen has passed her first cold night in her cold grave. She is buried in the Grange Cemetery and I took a careful note of the spot so that I may visit and ruminate over the many good points of that good woman. This morning I went to the Guild meeting at 10 a.m. There were seven present. I made some remarks. Afterwards I came up to G.'s and had a walk with John, Ned and Mick. It is a dull day. |
| Monday March 21 | It is a strange fact, yet fact it is nevertheless, that even in my saddest moments some funny thing appears in my mind and I have great difficulty in refraining from smiling. This is how I sometimes felt during the recent sad bereavement of Mrs. Gilbertson. This evening, I was up at Miss R.'s from 6 to 7:30 p.m. Had walk round the book stalls later. I felt like buying 100 pounds worth of books. My actual money possession was two pence so I postponed the purchases. |

Tuesday March 22	Wee Mag is ten months old today. It has been interesting to watch the progress she has made during that period. She now goes through the form of drying her face when she gets hold of the towel and her attempts to brush and comb her hair would provoke a smile from an owl. Tonight Liz, baby and I went to library.
Wednesday March 23	Co-operation is catching on in Edinburgh at least. In a bill I have (St. Cuthbert's) I see they have three big bakeries; one biscuit factory; three big stabling departments; one boot factory; five big tailoring, furnishing and jewellery departments; twenty-seven butcher shops; thirty-seven grocery departments; eighteen baking departments; seven coal departments; two drug stores; one painter shop; and a great big general work shop where numerous tradesmen are in their employment. This shows how far a workers' movement can go and still be progressing. Wee Mag was very heated and unwell today. In the afternoon Liz took her out and she came back quite herself again.
	In the evening, we visited Mack and my Aunt Jean at Gorgie Road. While there, Aunt Maggie came in. This is the first time I have seen her for about seven years. She gave baby 2/6.
Thursday March 24	Tonight at our Guild the debate was "Have we too many periodicals?" The affirmative was carried by 6:5. In a talk on Social Evils I pointed out to some of the members the fact that 50,000 children go breakfastless to school every morning in London. And that there are 75,000 prostitutes in that Town. These are evils with a vengeance! Our would-be social reformers never speak of them let alone tackle them.
Friday March 25	For several weeks I have been at Liz to sew my working trousers. Each evening I left them off for sewing; each morning I put them on unsewed. The excuse was always, "Oh, I did not remember." Last night I put them on the floor with a piece of paper whereon was this inscription, "Lest We Forget". It had the desired effect!

Saturday March 26	Last night I took baby out for a little airing. I went along by Slateford Road. She began to cry and I made for home. I am brave in my own way but I simply won't face a crowd with a crying baby. It is a great test of courage. This afternoon, Liz and I had a walk. We took baby out in the mail cart with us. We visited Gollogly's. Jim is ill and Hugh very poorly. I spoke to the latter for some time. Poor fellow. Some years ago he was a big stout fellow and now he had not strength to smoke his pipe. I felt his legs and they are very thin. Truly a great change indeed. We are weakly creatures! In the evening, I attended a *Crier* meeting when we discussed various subjects. I met an original old character named "Hunter", of whom more anon.
Sunday March 27	Before this week is past the first quarter of the year will have gone to join all past Time and so it is that Time is ever on the wing. The years slip in and then slip out and men slip away and scarcely know they have been alive. Time is fleeting. Life is short. Yet in life's short space men can accomplish much. How many men accomplish the limit? Very few indeed! I went to Guild this morning. This morning finished the session. In the afternoon we had Hadden to tea. In the evening, we had my cousin, Jeanie Forbes. This is my cousin's first visit to us.
Monday March 28	How very cheating the weather is to be sure. Today it was so dull that I thought it would rain any minute. However, it kept up until the evening. This evening, Liz and I went to the Store and I bought some ties. A present to Mr. William Forbes who is going to Canada. I bought a bookcase from him and nearly burst carrying it home in a shower.
Tuesday March 29	Some students wished to have a joke at the expense of their ill-natured professor. At midnight they went to his house and rang his bell. He came to his window. "Well?" he snarled. "We have come to tell you, Sir, that one of your windows is open." "Dear me! Which one?" "The one you are looking out, you old fool." They then dispersed.

Wednesday March 30	Here is a cat story I heard from a man: I had a cat once that was very fond of our baby. I never saw a cat so much attached to a body. It was seldom out of the cradle when baby was there and was continually purring and rubbing round the baby. When the baby turned ill that cat was in great distress and when the baby died it was nearly brokenhearted. After the funeral, we put the cradle up on a high shelf out of the way and a while after missed the cat. Nine months later, while cleaning the house, we took down the cradle and there was the cat's skeleton!! I am very simple but could not take in that lie. I think it as absurd as it is disgusting.
Thursday March 31	Some time ago, Cairns told me some miser stories. One was of an old shopkeeper who had a habit of leaving his hat on his counter. A man went in and while his back was turned slipped the old miser's hat into an empty box which stood on the counter. The man than had occasion to leave the village and was away twenty years. On coming back he visited the old miser whose first greeting was, "I never saw my hat after you left my shop the last time." "I put it in that box," and lifting the lid he took out the hat from where it had lain undisturbed for twenty years. I am not responsible for this story. Guild in evening when we were to hear an essay on Salisbury by Mr. F. Cunninghame. Owing to illness he did not come. We held a protracted committee meeting.
Friday April 1	This is the day on which we are reminded what we are the other 364. Mark Twain. This afternoon I wrote some lines on my winning the glass draught board. I intended going out with T.C.s but the night damped my ardour and if I had gone out it would have damped my skin. Result— T.C.s postponed.
Saturday April 2	A drizzly day. There was a great demonstration today protesting against Chinese labour in So. Africa. Despite the rain there was a good turn out of people. But sad to relate, there were more people at a local football match. In the evening visited McDermotts. In the afternoon, I went out with *Town Criers*. In the evening, I went out with house crier—our baby.

Sunday April 3	Today I went along and saw Jim G. He has had a bad attack of pleurisy but is now getting better. I also saw Hugh. Poor fellow! How he drags out his life is a marvel. I hope to see him better yet but have my sad doubts. In the afternoon, Liz, Baby and I went to McDermott's christening party. Later we visited our Aunt. In an interval in the afternoon, I went to our class.
Monday April 4	Our baby is now in her eleventh month and is progressing favourably. She can now stand when placed with her back to the bunker. At 6 o'clock I went up to Miss Robertson's for an hour's bookkeeping. I met Liz and had a walk at 7:15 p.m. What an intricate puzzle bookkeeping is to me. Indeed all figures are. I simply cannot make any headway with them.
Tuesday April 5	This afternoon Mrs. McDermott with her baby and her sister visited us. It is a fine baby. And I hope it may thrive and prove a blessing to them. It is a nice plump little girl and is their first-born alive. For a long time I was out every evening. I am gradually breaking off that and stay in some evenings. I will soon be quite domesticated.
Wednesday April 6	I am still making headway towards domestication. I was again in this evening. Liz went out for a 'few minutes'. As usual when she goes out for a few minutes, she came back after more than an hour had elapsed. I was left in charge of baby. She played quietly for a time when an evil thought took possession of her and she arranged to give me a bad half-hour. She started crying and I started soothing. She became worse and I put on her hat and took her out when she went to sleep.
Thursday April 7	This was the business meeting night of the Guild. I was elected assistant librarian with charge of over 1,800 books. A splendid collection! I wish I could remove them to 105 Dundee Street. The salary for this job is nothing a year, payable in advance. I am always coming in for good things.

Friday April 8	Tonight I attended and took the minutes at the usual business meeting of the Sons of Temperance. There was the usual flow of eloquence and blether from some of the members. There have been high winds and much rain since April came in.
Saturday April 9	Tonight I was at a party in Forbes'. Met to give Forbes a send-off previous to his departure for Canada and I was sad and sore oppressed, and no wonder, for did I not hear there some of the songs and some of the melodeon tunes that I so often heard sung and played by friends who are now gone. Can any one wonder at my sadness when "Father O'Flynn" was being sung? That song Gilby used to sing with such good-heartedness. And "Barney Take Me Home Again" which used to be Hughie's song. And now poor Hughie will soon be home. Home to the Home his wife went to just recently. All these things show us how fleet is everything in the world of change. This is a wild day, there being several snow storms during the day.
Sunday April 10	I have such a lot of writing to do and I have made up my mind to do it, and will perhaps not do half of it. I have to write to Mrs. Cockburn in America and business letters. This is another changeable day—shine one minute; rain the next.
Monday April 18	For some time this valuable literary work has been amissing and I have not been able to put down my immortal notes. And I have just found it under the leg of the room table acting as a steadier. This is awful! Today is Spring holiday and Liz, Teen, Jean, baby and I went to Cramond where we had a most enjoyable picnic on the banks of the Almond.

Tuesday April 19	There is always a little well of tenderness deep down in a man somewhere. Speaking some time ago with Forbes on his coming departure he said, "There will be the usual weeping and wailing but I regard it as nothing," or words to that effect. I had occasion to be at the station along with a crowd gathered to give him a send-off. And shaking hands with old friends, Forbes cried like a girl. He thought he wouldn't but one never knows what a pang it must be to part with the friends of a lifetime to go to a foreign land. I did not go out this (Tuesday) evening.
Wednesday April 20	Last Sunday I wrote two letters to *Echoes'* editor—also poetry. I visited Hadden and McDermott. This evening I again remained indoors—a regular housebird—and read a goodly portion of *Trilby*. At about 10 o'clock this evening we had a visit of Mrs. Finlayson and daughter asking Liz to take two days work. Visit and work welcomed. I have lost the library keys also my watch key. It seems I have got a key-losing disease. It is a good job I'm no musician as I fear I would lose the key often.
Thursday April 21	This evening I went to house in Braid Avenue where Liz was working. Baby was also there and amused herself all day by pulling the tail of a fox terrier-like dog in the house. We were home about 8 and I never went to the Guild as I feared to meet an angry Guild without the library keys.
Friday April 22	I have borrowed a watch key from Miller and immediately I have done so, I find my own in my waistcoat pocket. The "Sons" meeting in the evening. I was in and saw H. Gollogly. H. is lying dying fast, going the road of his dear wife and child. I stood and looked at him for a time and thought—well, I cannot put down here all I thought of this sturdy chap of just a few years back.

65

| Saturday April 23 | This is the first anniversary of Gilbey's funeral. What a lot has happened since that Saturday when we fell in behind the hearse and silently and mournfully followed our deceased friend to the Grange Cemetery. Helen is since gone. Mary is gone. Mary's baby is gone. Primrose is gone and Hugh is going. A terrible change indeed! And I feel it. |

Today I walked round the book stalls, and then attended meeting of the Vigilance Association. Home at 6:20 p.m. Had tea (the McDermott's were here) and was out with Liz, Jean and baby till about 9:30 p.m. It was drizzling rain.

| Sunday April 24 | This morning I took *Trilby* and went out for a short walk. I read through a good many of the pages and visited Hadden. Then home and had breakfast and finished *Trilby*. What a disgraceful record for a Sunday! In the afternoon I went to class, then to Forbes' in evening with Liz and baby. |

Today I found the library keys in my Sunday trousers pocket. I heaved a sigh of relief, for the circulation of free literature to the world can again go on.

| Monday April 25 | In the evening I went to Miss Robertson's for an hour's bookkeeping. While there an old lady came up to visit Miss R. and tell her of the death of her two birds. The cock died first and the hen half an hour after. I thought it was a broken heart had killed the hen, but it turned out a broken bill instead, through her pecking hard lump sugar! |

Monday May 2	Here I am a week back with my diary and must lose that week. This is my birthday. I am 29 years of age today and my wife has celebrated the event by giving me a nice pair of brown boots. I was up at Miss Robertson's for bookkeeping.

During last week Hugh Gollogly (Friday, April 29th) died, and on Sunday, May 1st was buried in the Grange Cemetery. This makes about seven deaths within thirteen months and four of them have consisted of two fathers and two mothers. One couple leaving five children and the other leaving three children. I attended Hugh's funeral, which was private. During the service at the graveside there was one "gentleman" stood with his hat on. It was a top hat and one generally looks for manners beneath a top hat. I don't. I reckon it a mark of refined ignorance and cultured insolence.

Tuesday May 3	Painting—I am a week previous.

Of all the seasons of the year, the least desirable is Spring as that is when spring cleaning begins—enough in itself to condemn any season. What a turmoil trying to place two beds, one table, and six chairs where there is hardly room for a table alone. And then if you are standing in the middle of the floor you cannot move an inch without going up against wet paint. A most excellent thing for removing wet paint is to lean up against it while it is wet.

Tonight I was out with Hadden learning him to cycle. I did some very hard running and was sweating as a result.

Wednesday May 4	I am a week previous, re painting.

Another evening among paint, and of all times this is surely the worst time a visitor could choose to come. My cousin, Jean Forbes, was in tonight. She is a nice girl. Our house is now nearly done, and tonight the bed recess not being dry yet after its dose of oil paint, we slept on a bed made on the floor. If our baby is to fall out of bed, she could not choose a better time as she would only have a fall of about four inches. The *Town Crier* should have been out, but owing to a dispute between the editor and the printer who refuses to print it, it is not out yet. It has been given to the Co-operative Press, Leicester, to print.

Thursday May 5	Today and this evening wee Maggie has had a touch of her mother's disease: ill temper. And it has been my job to nurse her this evening. Consequently I cannot get to the Guild, and I am slightly ill-tempered myself as a result, though it is not my nature to be. What an amiable chap I am! I am never angry unless something ruffles me.
Friday May 6	This evening Ned and I went to the "Sons" meeting. We had reports of the half-yearly meeting of the Executive Council. Each one speaking of it referred to the tea given them. A very important item it appears, is the tea. These past four days have been very wet. About a fortnight ago I wrote to *Echoes*—two letters and a piece of verse on the coming trip. I don't expect any of them will appear as I am only a coalman and not a grocer or a draper. This is my own foreman's opinion.
Sunday May 8	A wet day. I did not go out till afternoon when I went to class. Then I had a short walk along Princes Street. Raining. Met P. Welsh and went with him to G.'s. Home at 11:00 p.m.
Monday May 9	Tonight I again had to act as male nurse to our baby. She seems happy when she is keeping me in from an engagement. I should have been at Miss R.'s at 6 p.m. I went up at 8 p.m. and showed her the Guild photo. I also got one of the photos of the gymnastic class. I then went hunting the book stalls and farely waded through bargains of books without as much money in my pocket as would buy a farthing tract. The rich say the poor are happiest. At that rate I must be extremely happy.
Tuesday May 10	Now we are busying about the house cleaning. Liz has stripped the paper off the walls and the house does not look nice. We are all so busy and I am so useful that I don't know what to turn my hand to first and do nothing at all. About all I am fit for is breaking wood or poring over a book if I get the chance, which my wife sees that I seldom get. We had the top of the walls ochred tonight and some painting done.

Wednesday May 11	Again up to the neck in furniture and everything is upset besides my nerves. The remainder of the painting was done this evening with the exception of the doors. I was in attendance and again at a loss what to do and did nothing. When a man does nothing, he does nothing wrong. I do nothing very well. I am a champion at doing nothing.
Thursday May 12	Met Mr. Cairns and went with him to Guild. A fortnight ago, Mr. Cairns told me about a precentor who got up to sing a hymn beginning:

"The hour of my departure's come,
I heard the voice that calls me home . . ."

then he fell down and expired. What a blessed thing it must be to die in a church. I don't envy it for all that. I prefer to live outside the church than die inside it.

Friday May 13	This evening I took John Imrie to the "Gardeners" when he joined the Myrtle. It was pouring rain when the meeting came out. There were eight new members joined. I wish I could see the same numbers coming up to the "Sons".
Saturday May 14	This morning the sun was shining when I went out at 6 a.m. At about 7 a.m. it was raining. After that the sun again showed himself and gave promise of a beautiful day, when lo and behold at about 10 a.m. there came on a sunny shower which lasted about an hour and a half and drenched many things including some coalmen.

The shepherd saw the young man fold his love to his manly bosom. He sighed and said, "Who will I fold?" "You can go and fold the sheep," was the young man's reply.

Liz, baby and I were out in the evening. Called at Crans in High Street. They were out and we went to G.'s. Today I had a bath, a shave and my hair cut. This was almost too much for one day.

Sunday May 15	This is a fine morning and the sun is shining in the Heavens—a proper place for it—where else could it shine from? I read a goodly portion of Ian MacLaren's *Bonnie Brier Bush*. It gives one a grand idea of the old-fashioned "Unco' Guid", and their wrestlings with the Evil one. In the afternoon we—Liz, baby and I—met Aunt Jean and McDermott in Gorgie Road. Forbes' later.
Monday May 16	'Twas ever thus, he who has most gets most. Today Tom who had plenty of caps got two more from a woman. I have just one and got none. Later I came off smiling with one of Tom's two. We have just received a letter from Cardiff, Ma'am and Dad. Miss R.'s at 6 p.m. Met Liz and baby at 7:30 p.m.
Tuesday May 17	G.'s at night. Had some bookkeeping from Jim. Also some books. Later we had a walk together. I am not good at arithmetic bookkeeping but lend me a book and you will find me a master at book-keeping. I have many apt pupils with my circle of friends. The worst of it is they are keeping my books.
Wednesday May 18	They say a razor should get a rest. I would be only too glad to give mine a forty-year rest if I could only get another to fill its place. I have just come through the ordeal of shaving with it. Hence these remarks. I was in the Empire tonight with Cran and Ned. Lord Chief Justice to Boy who is a witness in Court. "Do you know what an oath is?" Boy: "Yes, Sir. I was your caddie."
Thursday May 19	For nearly two years I have had nothing in *Echoes*. This month I again appear with a poem and a letter. To both of these efforts the editor adds some veiled insolence. There is also a reply to Tom's letter of last month. A minister speaking of one of those fire and brimstone books of his youth quoted the following, "Reader, you may be dead before you read this book." "And it is very likely I will," added the minister, "as that is forty years ago and I am not yet through it and not likely to be." This evening I wrote a golf song. I know as much about golf as I do about the theory of music.

Friday May 20	This evening I met Jim G. in back of Castle and went up to "Sons" together. We later heard the Cadets' concert which follows their business. One fellow sang "Mary" in a voice that would have suited the Music Hall.
Saturday May 21	I have been very busy all this week and have not found time to do my bookkeeping lesson. This afternoon I went out with *Town Crier*s. I met a wholesale agent's man who criticised the T.C. editor. What brave some people are where there is no danger! In the evening I was out with Liz and baby and Cousin Jean Forbes. We saw the finish up of the London to Edinburgh Motor Cycle Race. They finished up at the General P.O.
Sunday May 22	An old man who until recently worked in the Coal Depot told me that all poets are mad. He did not know that I dabbled a little in verses. I did not dispute with the man, but the irony of the whole thing is that the old man is now in the asylum and the poets are still on the outside of that institution.
Monday May 23	I am still plodding away with bookkeeping. I am making but slow progress. I was at Miss Robertson's again this evening. Met Liz and baby and went walk.
Tuesday May 24	This is a holiday. We are celebrating the birthday of a dead Queen. Why make a difference between her and other dead Queens? If we must celebrate the birthday of one, why not the lot? That would run us in for a holiday nearly every day. Commercialism would then have to take a back seat, but then we would be celebrating the birthdays of Queens and when not doing that we could get by doing each others washing. This morning I was out at a flitting from 5 till 7:45 a.m. The rest of the day I wasted, then I helped Mrs. Logan to flit at night.
Wednesday May 25	This afternoon while I was coming home from work I met a man who was very like Gilbey. But I knew he was not Gilbey. He roams these parts no more. Alas!

Thursday May 26	This afternoon it was very warm. In the evening I finished the papering of Mrs. Logan's rooms. I then went and helped Tom McD. to flit. After that I assisted in shifting the rest of Mrs. Logan's things and altogether put in rather a warm evening. I was tired out when I got to bed at 12 o'clock.
Friday May 27	I thought I was done with the flitting season and gave thanks accordingly. When I returned from a walk with Liz I got the job to remove a bed, bedding, and several other things from 68 Temple Park Crescent to Gibson Terrace. I withdrew the aforementioned thanks and went up with a heavy heart. This evening while Liz and I were out we met the Rev. Mr. Scott, the assistant minister at our marriage. He is a very nice young man and is very gentle.
Saturday May 28	This afternoon Tom, Miller and I were at a flitting. When done we got a cup of tea and a corned beef sandwich. In the evening, Mr. Sidney was in and told us what a harmless cat he has. "It won't kill anything," he said. "If a louse bites him he will take it out and caution it and put it back again." Tom and I went to *Town Crier* meeting later.
	It was pouring rain all through the night and morning. When I looked out the window this morning I saw a massive-looking black thing. I thought I had discovered a great mammoth but it turned out to be a flitting with a tarpaulin over it.
Sunday May 29	Today I wrote a letter to editor Taylor. Also a golf song. Taylor said in reply to a letter of mine regarding the blaring of the band during meal times in a hall, that I should take little bits of cotton wool with me. A truly absurd statement. Imagine half the excursionists going about the town with cotton wool in their ears, and all through a band which they pay to add to our amusement. I was up at Annie's during the day. Had a talk with Donald, my brother. Also at Tom's. At class at 5 p.m.

Monday May 30	The letter that I wrote for Taylor I have very successfully lost. I visited Mr. Cairns and showed him my golf song. He said it was quite on a par with my other pieces. I was shown all over their new house and got some picture frames and Macaulay's *Biography* from him. I should have been at Miss Robertson's for bookkeeping but owing to the baby not being well I was detained and goodness knows! I cannot afford to lose any time over it.
Tuesday May 31	This month has now finished. In this month many important personages have been born, but the most important birth that ever took place during all the Mays since time began was my own birth. That is as far as I am concerned, at any rate!
Wednesday June 1	Now begins the sixth month of the year. How the time flies. Soon will another half-year and then the whole year be gone. And thus it is the lives of mortals pass and then we enter Eternity where we will no longer live by hours, days, months and years but go on through Eternity. What an awful thing to think of is Eternity! Who can fathom it? I was at G.'s at night.
Thursday June 2	I was again at G.'s in evening. Ned was to come with me to Dalmeny St. but couldn't, being too busy. I was at Guild later. After the Guild closed I listened to a lady playing the violin and singing for coppers in Bread St. She was a splendid musician but was not getting much remuneration.
Friday June 3	This morning Bailie Waterson died. He was not very consistent but he was still a good man and his loss will be greatly felt not only in the Council but throughout the city. Brief tributes were paid to him in our "Son's" meeting this evening. I visited Bro. Dickman this evening and reported result to the meeting.
Saturday June 4	Today Liz bought a new costume. It looks very well on her and she looks very well in it, so that with two very well everything is very well indeed. It was a very hot day and I being naturally tired—some people call it laziness— but that is owing to their lack of culture—I felt like sitting down in many a place where there was no seat.

F

Sunday June 5	All is bustle and stew at our house! 'Cos why? We are going to church. And this is an event that does not take place very often. I noticed a crack in the church wall and was afraid it would give way at that part Dr. MacGregor asked a blessing on the Righteous Mission at present in Tibet where the British are slaughtering the natives in cold blood. Call you that Righteousness?
Monday June 6	This afternoon I was at the funeral of Bailie Waterson. I never saw such a big turnout at a funeral. The feature of it was, I think, the turn of the poor children. Many of them barefooted and in rags, yet with as much and perhaps more respect than many who wore the Council gown of "guid braid claith". The streets were thronged with people who lifted up their hats to the Provost and to the hearse.

Miss Robertson's later.

Tuesday June 7	I have about five different places to go to this evening and as I could not go to all of them I decided on going to none. So stayed at home and rested my right foot which is badly swelled. I was along at Mr. Sydney's for a while during the evening. I have lost my purse's contents. 8d I think. I did not go into hysterics over it as there is no use crying over spilt coppers.
Wednesday June 8	My foot is still sore. I read a small book on Lady Nairne, the Scottish songstress. She wrote "The Laird of Cockpen", "Land o' the Leal", "Rowan Tree", "Hundred Pipers" and numerous others. She kept secret her powers as a poetess. I did not like the book. I was along to Mr. Sydney's in the evening. There has been a cold east wind blowing all day and my eyes have suffered in consequence. It is now dull and cold and a great change from yesterday which was very warm.

Thursday June 9	Some time ago I urged on a young man the importance of joining a Friendly Society. He simply giggled and laughed at the mention of it. He is now ill and his first day's illness cost him 6/—Doctor 2/6, medicine 3/6. I think he will join a society when he is strong again.
	Tonight I was at the Guild. We sold our sofa tonight. Our baby is now running about. She is now off our hands a bit, but we have to watch her. Her chief delight is when the dresser door is open to get pulling at the dishes. When she breaks the most valuable one among them her heart rejoices. Tonight it is bitter cold with sharp east wind blowing.
Friday June 10	On May 28th last the public houses started their early closing at 10:00 p.m. It seems strange to see them closing at that hour.
Saturday June 11	Mr. and Mrs. McDermott, Liz, baby and I went to the Gardens in the afternoon and heard the Black Rifles Band play. In the evening Liz went to the Store to buy a blouse. I waited outside with the baby. They say everything comes to those who wait. That is true if they wait long enough. I think Liz was the last to come out of the Store. In fact, I was beginning to think they had put her away in the safe and I would not see her at all. Later we went to G.'s. The class picnic was held today; they had good weather and enjoyed themselves.
Sunday June 12	I was to have been out at 11:00 a.m. this morning. I got out at 2:00 p.m. That is a small sample of my Sunday punctuality. We went up to see the Catholic Procession but as baby kicked up a row we had to come away just several minutes before the time, 4:00 p.m. I was at the class at 5 p.m. This winds up the season. Miss Robertson finished her discourse by telling us to place our trust in the Rock of Ages after which we sang "Jesus Lover of My Soul". We were at Aunt Jean's later.
Monday June 13	Tom is on holiday. It is raining this morning. That is just Tom's luck. Liz is up at the Dental Hospital having two teeth taken out. She slept none all night. I was down at the Grassmarket and heard Miller & Richard's Band. It was painful to listen to them. G.'s later.

75

Tuesday June 14	Today, I wrote to Queen, editor of the *Town Crier*. I gave him a severe criticism. I also sent a letter to Taylor, editor of *Echoes*. I am getting on indeed when I write letters to two real live editors in one day—and criticising them, too. Tom was down this evening and we went to Hadden's together. Lizzie's face is sore and swollen today. I got Forbes "Diary of a journey" which is a record of the events of his voyage to Canada. I am reading it.
Wednesday June 15	Liz has still a swollen jaw. The result of dental stress. She has a big washing on today. And the baby is going about holding onto her tails and altogether a working woman has a pretty hot time of it. Of course, she might have been a mayoress or duchess if she had cared to. So some of our gentry tell us. Of course, I have got by the stage for believing that, thanks to R. Blatchford.
Thursday June 16	I should have been at the Guild this evening but stayed at home and did a bit of painting. I had a nine-page letter from Queen. He was sorely put about at the tone of my letter. I showed it to Tom McD. and Hadden.
Friday June 17	Today I wrote to Queen in answer to his letter of yesterday. I also went to meeting of "Sons". The room is now looking very well. We have got the sofa out of the road. I finished the painting and got to bed some little time after 11 p.m. What a busy mortal I am in the house! I am very handy if there are any sticks to break or even things that are not wanted broken, I can break. I am in my element when breaking anything. Perhaps that accounts for me always being 'broke' myself.
Saturday June 18	This day concludes Tom's holidays. I have had a country lad working with me in his stead. A big strong lad with a grand knowledge of "coos, ho-arses, 'neeps an' ither things". We were at the gardens this afternoon and heard the band. In the evening we visited Aunt Jean and the Brydon's, Gorgie. Today our room is cleaned up and as I was in it today I thought myself not badly off with such a nice little room and kitchen, and a nice baby, and a wife who only quarrels at times.

Sunday June 19	This forenoon I was out early. I visited several friends including G.'s and Hadden. In the evening Liz and I were at Forbes'. This was a fine day although the wind is cold at times.
Monday June 20	There is only one topic at our work today. It is the Trip which takes place tomorrow. We are looking forward to a good day. There are 1,800 going. This number is a record, I think, for the Store. In the evening I went up to talk with Queen but he was out. Afterwards went and heard the Band in the Grassmarket. Home at 9:20 p.m.
Tuesday June 21	All is astir at our house this morning. Liz wanted me to rise ere it was yet 4 a.m. and all this fuss to catch a train that leaves at 7 a.m. We left the house at about 5:50 a.m. and along with Jim G. and Ned's wife, we got down to the Waverley in good time. We left at 7 a.m. and were in Arbroath at 9 a.m. The sun was shining and it remained so all day. We had a first-class holiday and enjoyed ourselves immensely. Wee Maggie's face was much sunburnt. We were at home at 8 p.m. It was chilly in Edinburgh.
Wednesday June 22	Again the topic at our work today is the excursion. Those who were not there are anxious to hear all about it and those who were there are anxious to tell all about it. One man bought a bunch of Arbroath smokies and on opening his parcel to his better half, he found it to contain sausages. Some other person would be opening a parcel of sausages and be surprised to find smokies.
Thursday June 23	If I were as full of good actions as I am of good intentions, my triumphant entry into Heaven would be certified. But the spirit is willing and the flesh is weak. Tonight I intended going to the Guild and fulfilling my duties as assistant librarian there, but on getting into the good company of Ned and Jim, the intention was cancelled. We had a walk together and talked on many subjects beginning with dear knows what and ending with religion.

Friday June 24	Another good intention off. I intended going along early to Jim's and having a lesson on bookkeeping when I got along and discovered that he had gone to the Empire Theatre. I also set off for that place and booked a seat in the gallery. They are certainly the highest seats in the theatre. Jim must have been in the lower seats as I never saw him in the gallery. R. G. Knowles was chief turn. He was very good. "John Johns, aged 24 years. Weight 28 stone. Died, etc.": "Open wide ye Golden Gates". People do awfully silly things nowadays. Imagine putting a fence around a cemetery. People who are outside don't want in the those inside can't get out. There are two of his many jokes. Badly told, of course.
Saturday June 25	Today is all bustle and hurry. 'Cos why? We are all going down to the jumble sale in the Grassmarket. What a rabble! People clamouring for bargains. I was in the middle of it intending to purchase a suite of furniture, several ladies dresses and a suit of clothes and a good overcoat for about 1/6 the lot. 'Twas all the cash I had I need scarcely say. I did not make those purchases but came away with a nine-penny poets for one penny. In the evening I had a look round the bookstalls and was fairly in my element. Result? No purchases. G.'s later. The young folks were all out!
Sunday June 26	This morning I was out early and had wee Mag with me giving her the benefit of the fresh air and the lovely morning's beauty. Liz dressed and went to church and heard a memorial service to a deceased grocer and spirit merchant. "And everyone in the church wept," said Liz. Fancy that for a whisky seller! I went up to McD.'s, Sydney's after tea. Then Mr. and Mrs Miller's later. The Millers are a young married couple who have come to neighbour us. There was a man there who knew a whole lot of other men with a joke connected to each of them. If it was a good joke, he himself was the hero.

Monday June 27	There is a newly married couple living next to us and they are in a great state because they have lost their cat. I remember when we were first married, we had a kitten which would not keep out of the bed. I wanted it kept out. Liz said to let it stay in. In the middle of the night I laid hold of it and under the impression that Liz was asleep I threw it across the floor, when bang, bang, I felt Liz starting an unprovoked assault on my ribs. She was lying wide awake.
	In the evening, Tom and I went to the band in the Grassmarket. Met the G.'s there. I went to Parker's later.
Tuesday June 28	G.'s again this evening. We were along seeing the inspection of the City Volunteers. They were very slow in their movements. Their attempts to be smart were almost as funny to witness as the officer's attempts at military dignity. Heaven help this thriving nation if it had to depend on its volunteers. I remember some years ago seeing some young gents being put through some drills by regular sergeants at the Castle Esplanade. Their attempts were painful to witness and when I heard that they were volunteer officers my feeling may be better imagined than described.
Wednesday June 29	Some time ago I made up my mind to go in for a strict study of arithmetic. I have not yet started. So much for my good resolution. I was to go along to G.'s this evening but my foot is very sore and I am giving it a rest. I was at the band this evening. It was the Black Watch but I did not like their programme. The music elicited cheers at intervals from many whom I don't credit with a musical education. Of course, it is a sign of culture to cheer high class music which only about one tenth of the audience understands. And if we have not the culture, well, we can pretend we have.
Thursday June 30	My foot is again sore. This is the result of a sprain I got while playing football about thirteen years ago. It has troubled me at intervals. The weather has been very warm today. I am looking forward to my holidays which come on next week. I am going to Rome not far from home.

79

Friday July 1	Six months today will be New Year's Day. The year is now half gone. I don't hear people wishing each other a Happy Half New Year. I am still looking forward to a glorious week of laziness next week. That is the worker's holiday. Not to Nice nor Venice where his employers go to. Of course, he can go to Rome about the doors. The weather has been splendid all this week.
Saturday July 2	
Monday July 4	This morning I was up first as usual. Liz lay extra long in bed and I was wondering is it my holidays or hers? We left the house after 11 a.m. and went along and met Mrs. E.G., Mary Ann G. and wee Mick. We met Ned at Waterloo Place where we took the car at 12:20 p.m. for good old Portobello. We enjoyed ourselves fairly well until 3 p.m. when it began to rain heavily. We took the car home. This evening, I got a p.c. from Queen asking for contributions for this month's issue, this evening if possible. I promptly wrote a piece of prose and a piece of verse and as promptly lost the prose. I also visited Bro. Parker.
Tuesday July 5	Some time ago I promised a friend in America that I would visit Liberton and see her son's grave there. I fixed on this day for the fulfillment of that promise. Accordingly, Liz, wee Peg and I took the car and then walked the remainder to that delightful little place in the early afternoon. A quaint, old neglected-looking churchyard it is. On our homecoming, we saw a Salvation Army funeral. An impressive sight! Later we went to St. Cuthbert's Sports then my Aunt's in Gorgie Road.
Wednesday July 6	"The best laid schemes o' mice and men gang aft agley." Today we had planned for a picnic at Barnton. We were just going to set out with our basketfull of sandwiches, etc. when there started a steady downpour of rain and the Gods be thanked. I was spared. I would have been the only mere man amongst seven women. This was half my holidays over.

Thursday July 7	All is stir and bustle in spite of the fact that it is my holidays and Liz is busy over the washing tub. I thought to have escaped it and got out on my own but no. I had the parental duty of watching baby to do and sweating over the wringer—and this is my holidays! I was at the Guild in the evening. A lawyer's letter came to me today re my mother.
Friday July 8	For the first time in my week's holidays I lay long in bed this morning. This forenoon I visited my Aunt Lizzie and James G. re lawyer's letter of yesterday. I got about ten advices all different and came home and acted on my own. In the afternoon I went again to Liberton when I wrote a piece of verse by the graveside of Mr. C.'s son. I wrote another piece on my way home to a plant I had taken from his grave. G.'s in the evening.
Saturday July 9	Today winds up my holidays. Liz and I went out together in the forenoon. We visited a Curiosity Exhibition—admission 1d—hence the visit. In the afternoon a party of us held a picnic at Barnton. The party was not all to my liking but on the whole I enjoyed the outing. There were children's picnics there and I was much interested in their races. Beauty was also rampant in very light dresses. We got home at 10:40 p.m. and found this inscription on our door: "Done a moonlight; Gone but not forgotten." This was a trick of a neighbour.
Sunday July 10	My holidays are over. On the whole they have been enjoyable as I have had at least leisure for the week. I feel lazier than ever and that is saying something to go back to my work. In the evening, Liz went to Forbes'. I went a walk along Princes Street and then met the G.'s in Lothian Road. Home and dismally prepared for bed in the full knowledge that I had to go to work in the morning. A very disheartening thought.
Monday July 11	Started work. Felt out of form a bit. Will just have to get used to it again. In the evening I went with some friends to the Exhibition where we heard a lecture: "Historic Edinburgh". It was one of the most interesting lectures I have heard. I saw the handwriting of Burns and Scott and many other curious things.

81

Tuesday July 12	This evening I had a walk round the bookstalls where I saw many books that I would have liked to possess at prices ranging from 1 penny to 1 pound. I bought a penny one.
	I went out with Miller's cycle later and gave Tom a lesson. He could almost ride in a short time. Tom and I went to the Young Scots meeting later. I had several arguments and Tom had one with the chief speaker.
Wednesday July 13	Our baby is now up to all sorts of mischief and just a few minutes ago she went from the room into the kitchen. Her mother came in and got her with a tin of condensed milk at her mouth. She was covered all over the nose and mouth with it and was smacking her lips.
	Today I heard that the *Town Crier* was stuck. Spent the evening with the G.'s.
Thursday July 14	This is the shopkeepers' holiday and the town has a Sunday appearance without the church bells, of course. Last night I brought home models of a parlour suite made with different colours of glass beads. The suite has been put together by a little blind girl and consists of ten pieces costing only 2/-. Some of the works of the blind are truly marvellous! The Royal Blind have for some years had a splendid brass band.
	I went to the Guild in the evening.
Friday July 15	There has been a row in our locality. A little girl next door to us has got a doll and our wee Peg wanted to know the reason why she had not a doll. The affair was settled by Liz buying a doll for her.
	Nell Forbes, Willie Forbes and John Bell—Nell's fellow—started for Canada this morning. Half-yearly meeting of the "Sons" tonight. One of the brothers led in the singing of a verse of song. He pitched too high and broke down amid confusion. It was funny.

Saturday July 16	Today I called on my mother on my way home from my work. Liz would not come out with me in the afternoon. I went down to "Gardener's" and heard the 7th Lancers' Band. Met G.'s there. In the evening I again met Jim and Ned and went and heard a lecture on "Historic Edinburgh" by Prof. Baldwin Brown. It was very interesting and many views of the ancient buildings of Edinburgh were thrown on the screen. He deplored the disappearance of many of those old places during recent years. Jim, Ned & I had a walk down the Cowgate & up the High Street later.
Sunday July 17	This forenoon Ned and I had a walk together when we visited many of the old scenes of pictures which were thrown on the screen yesterday evening in the lecture. How I longed for an historical education. I was home at 2 p.m. Out again with Liz and wee Peggy and John Forbes to Merchiston Cemetery where we visited the graves of the Edens, my Uncle Thomas and my grandfather of my own name. Liz, baby and I had a walk in the evening. We were in the gardens, Princes Street, where wee Mag lost a small broken knife I have had for years.
Monday July 18	It is funny to watch children at play. Last evening in the Gardens, on wee Mag being put down on the grass, she got her eye on a wee chap of I think about eighteen months. They became fast friends, wee Mag giving him a nice biscuit and getting as a reward a halfpence from the child's father. No man is ever so constantly employed as when his wife is washing the baby and he is attending her. She sits down without nearly everything. I marvel at her remembering the water and the baby! I had a short walk with Tom, then came home and we both did some writing.

Tuesday July 19	This morning I was dozing about the house in my own and every other body's way. Ned G. came in and asked me to accompany him on a cycle ride. I got permission from the wife and set off to Ned's home where I learned it was a drive they were doing. It was a male affair; seven of us. We went to Compensation Ponds and had a most enjoyable day. We were there five years ago when there were about thirty-six of us, both sexes. Oh, that happy lot of young folks, alas! Several are dead—Gilbey, Hugh, Helen and Wm. Primrose all having gone to their rest beyond the tomb.
Wednesday July 20	This morning a young woman of our acquaintance named Mrs. Hardy died after giving birth to her first baby. She was not yet out of her teens. This afternoon an old man was rapping at the door of one of our neighbours. I went out to speak to him. He had left Craiglockhart Poorhouse that morn at 9 o'clock and had taken until now—5 p.m.—to come here, during which time he had not had anything to eat. He had come in search of his son who, however, had left that house eighteen months ago. He was downhearted on hearing this but was glad to come into my house where I got him some spirits and gave him some tea. I then went and found his son and took the old man to him. Spent the evening very enjoyably with Mr. Cairns at his home.
Thursday July 21	"Oh, man, it's an awfu' job when a body has tae gang tae the Puirhoose at ma time o' life," so said the old man to me last evening. Poor old soul! He does not know that it is more than a pity—it is a swindle. I was at the Guild in the evening. Cairns told me this joke: A priest seeing an Irishman going into a pub called on him without Pat taking the least notice. On coming out, the priest said, "Didn't you hear me, Pat?" "I did, your reverence, but I had only two pence and that was no use for the two of us."
Friday July 22	I have been out till late every evening for a fortnight and I am at present tired out and treating myself to a night at home. Liz is making her second attempt at weaning wee Mag. She is fourteen months old today and is being lively. She is generally first child in our backyard at play in the morning and I have seen her out of doors after 10 p.m.

Saturday July 23	This is the Trade's Holiday Saturday. I was working this morning till 9:30 a.m. Liz, baby and I spent the afternoon enjoyably at Portobello. We went and came by car. Edinburgh is well off with such a fine place in its neighbourhood. There are two sets of pierrots performed daily on the beach. Our neighbours, Miller, had tickets for a trip to Aberdeen today. The train left at 6:15 a.m. They were newly out of bed at that minute. Result: Train well on its way to Aberdeen while they were well on their way to the station.

Sunday July 24	This has been a disagreeable day. This forenoon I had a walk with Ned. We saw some of the Volunteers returning from camp. In the afternoon, Liz, baby and I went to Forbes'. In the evening, I had a walk along Princes Street, then came back to Lothian Road where Ned and I listened to the preachers.

Monday July 25	Wee Maggie has seen a doll in the hands of another child. Consequently there has been a row that has only been put right by the putting of a new doll—brand new, 6d.—in her hand. This is fully ten minutes ago and the doll is not yet broken.

I did not go out this evening.

Tuesday July 26	This evening I accompanied . . .

My Aunt and Cousin Jean were up from Gorgie this evening.

As Forbes' house is nearly empty, the tea party of Maggie's presentation was held at our house this afternoon. There was a sing-song and a lot of handshaking at the end. It rained very heavily all the afternoon and evening.

Thursday	All is hurry and bustle now with the Forbes'. In two days they will be gone. Their house is nearly cleared out and they are taking their meals at our house. None will miss them so much as my wife.

Friday August	Today we have two strangers in the house. They are a cat in a basket and a parrot in a cage. They belong to Forbes and are going with them to the distant land of Canada. Tomorrow, Forbes will be gone. Tonight I attended a meeting of the "Sons" to consider what steps should be taken to make our meetings more attractive. It was agreed to form a syllabus of debates and essays. I have to write an essay on Robert Fergusson, poet.
Saturday August	This morning I went up to Forbes' and bade them good-bye. And now they are gone! Liz went down to the station and saw them away. In the evening, Liz and I had a walk. G.'s at night—Liz and I.
Sunday August	Today I was busy with Fergusson. I intend putting a short article on him into *Echoes*. It is not such an easy matter. It is not the writing only but the reading up of the subject that takes the time.
Monday August	This evening I was again busy with Fergusson. I am nearly finished with it. When in St. Andrew's University, the bursars had to take their turn to ask a blessing on the meals which were noted for the sameness. With great solemnity Fergusson said:

> For rabbits hot and for rabbits cold,
> For rabbits young and for rabbits old,
> For rabbits tender and for rabbits tough
> Our thanks we render, for we've had enough.

This had the desired effect and there was a marked falling off in rabbits after that!

Tuesday Aug. 30	Like the active chap I am, I have not my article ready and it should be in the editor's hand by now. I am busy condensing it. It is a whole lot of good stuff and I am at a loss what to leave out.
Wednesday Aug. 31	This evening I went up to Cairns for his approval or non-approval of my short article. He said it was the best I have yet done and with some slight alterations he said it was fully good enough for *Echoes*. I came home and re-wrote it and posted it at 10:20 p.m.

Sunday Sept. 4	Today I attended a big procession of the Temperance Societies. We assembled in St. Andrew's Square and walked along Princes Street to Central Hall, Tollcross, where we had a fine service. In the evening Tom McD. and I went to the Meadows.
Monday Sept. 5	This is Fergusson's birthday. This evening Liz and I were out. We visited Andrews. I saw a street musician this evening send a boy up to a pawnshop with a handkerchief full of coppers. He got it changed and I noticed a one pound note amongst it. Not bad for a day's fiddle scraping.
Tuesday Sept. 6	G.'s at night. Had walk with Jim and Ned. Met Parker in High Street. Long talk with him as usual when I go to G.'s. I got home at 11.05 p.m.
Wednesday Sept. 7	Meeting at the foot of Murdoch Terrace very successful and a good crowd. Gunn spoke.
Thursday Sept. 8	Out of five weeks I have only been once to the Guild. This is the kind of attendance a married man keeps. "He stands between love and duty." We got a post card from Forbes' today saying that they were nearing their destination. We were at Aunt Forbes' this evening.
Friday Sept. 9	What an amount of books are in our public libraries! Great rows of the works of the world's greatest men. How I love books. Lamb says, "Give me an old book." I expect that is because he could not afford a new book which same fact accounts for so many old books in my own bookcase. In the evening I went from the library to the "Sons" meeting. One night recently I had a walk round the book stalls. I lifted and laid books with the air of one who would buy up the whole stock on a moment's notice. But there was no fear of that as my pockets were starving, and my purse? I had none!

Saturday Sept. 10	I used to hear my mother say, "This is the day that makes the lame and the lazy jump." This afternoon I thought I'd have an hour to write. I got my books and was going to write something about Fergusson when I heard, "Come on, Will, are you ready?" The books were then laid aside and I proceeded to get ready. We put in our Store checks then went up to the South Bridge. I showed Liz a cheap fish shop and she went and paid 2d. for a half mackerel. So much for the cheapness of that man's fishy wares. We got home all right after having our usual quarrel on the way. Today we had letters from Aggie Crighton and Mr. Stephenson. I was much surprised on receiving the latter's letter as I thought he had "thrown me over".
Sunday Sept. 11	What a lovely morning! I have been out for a short walk. There is a slight chilliness in the air now and the birds seem to have a mournful chirp as if they dreaded the hard times that the winter brings to them and poor people. I went in to the Infirmary and saw Gibson. He is now getting well. The forenoon I took up with writing and the evening Liz and I and baby spent at G.'s.
Monday Sept. 12	It is not often I give myself a treat but this evening at great sacrifice I spent a tanner on the Lyceum Theatre. Edward Terry, the great comedian was there in "The House of Burnside". A splendid play and well acted. This was followed by "Bardell v. Pickwick" from Dickens. This piece loses a lot of its humour on the stage. I enjoyed myself very much.
Tuesday Sept. 13	This afternoon I met Ned and Jim and had a walk along Princes Street. In the evening, Liz went to Lyceum while I stayed at home and watched the baby. I had Tom McDermott and Ned and Jim as visitors and again enjoyed the evening very well.

Wednesday Sept. 14	This evening I wrote to Aggie Crighton, Dundee, and Maud Robin, Cork. I then went to meeting of S.D.F. at foot of Murdoch Terrace. There the speaker, H. Sinclair, spoke in favour of "State Maintenance of School Children", and told us of 72 per cent of the children of one Edinburgh school with something wrong with them.
Thursday Sept. 15	This evening I went along to G.'s and then to the Guild. There was a record-breaking attendance, only myself being present. I met Ned, Jim and Frank and had a walk with them. Some time ago, a friend of mine was going on to a car. There was also a woman with four children going on. A young "lady" and "gentleman" also going on pushed the woman and bairns aside and boarded the car in front of them. Manners? Oh, Edinburgh!
Friday Sept. 16	This is a red-letter day in my life. *Echoes* contains a short article of mine on Robert Fergusson. I had had prose printed before but this is my most serious effort and I am more than pleased to see it in print. I will receive payment for it which is a great consideration with a poor man.
	This afternoon I intended doing a lot of writing. The afternoon is now nearly gone. It is now 5 p.m. and this note is all the writing I have done. If you want me to do a deal of writing, well give me a very little time and I'll manage. But give me six months to write an essay and I will sleep till about the last week and then do it.
	Out with the G.'s in the evening.
Saturday Sept. 17	The most of this afternoon I intended giving up to pen exercise. I have not yet had the pen in my hand today. My Aunt Lizzie is unwell. My wife went along to help her with the house work. I followed with baby and there's an afternoon gone. I have received praise on my effort in *Echoes*.
Tuesday Sept. 20	Wee Peg is very flushed today. I went up for the Dr. He came down later. I met and had talk with Wm. Queen. The Dr.'s advice is that wee Peg is to be kept indoors. This is rather difficult advice to follow. I paid 8d. for a bottle of medicine prescribed for her.

G

Wednesday Sept. 21	Today Peg is again running about and is very busy breaking the Dr.'s advice. She was on her swing. She does her own counting: she never gets beyond number two. She must have been nearly up to two thousand while she was still saying, "One, two, one, two!" I should not like to wait until she counted twenty. The Dr. visited today.
Thursday Sept. 22	Wee Peg is not so well today. She is still more flushed. She is always most ill at nights. The Dr. again came today. I visited the G.'s this evening. I am thinking of attending the Heriot Watt College this session. I will take as a subject "English Literature and Composition".
Friday Sept. 23	Wee Peg still ill. The cause of the trouble is the eye teeth coming through. I was at the "Sons" meeting this evening.
Saturday Sept. 24	The little robin is again heard warning us of the coming winter. In the cold and in the gloom his is ever a cheerful note. About ten years ago while lying in bed one Sunday morning, I heard the robin. I got up and wrote some verses on his cheery song. That was my first effort at verse. I was told lately that I have not yet improved on that effort.
	Wee Peg is still unwell and is kept indoors yet. I wish I saw her again all right. Liz is in a great state about her, although the Dr. says there is no danger.
Sunday Sept. 25	Wee Peg is not so heated today but is still kept indoors. She looks longingly towards the door at times but nature demands this imprisonment. Besides it is getting too cold for her to be out at play. Poor wee Peg, What would I not give to see you again all right!
Tuesday Sept. 27	I am busy writing an article on Wm. Cobbett. I intend it for *Echoes*.
Saturday Oct. 1	Today I spoke to editor of *Echoes*, a Mr. Stevenson. I gave him the Cobbett article with a promise to conclude it next month.

Monday Oct. 3	G.'s in evening. With Jim's advice—and Jim's money—I went up to Heriot Watt College. After that I went with Jim and Ned to Operetta House and saw the Animated Pictures. A poor evening's entertainment. Wee Peg is much better today.
Tuesday Oct. 4	This evening I went up to Cairns and gave him *Echoes*. I also got him to look over my essay on Fergusson which he said he would do. I have to read it to the Sons of Temperance and the Guild. Cairns says it will do and that is an improvement on my last essay—Wm. Cobbett. I am a great literateur! No wonder I walk with lightsome tread and condescendingly look on drs., editors, etc.
Wednesday Oct. 5	I went up to Heriot Watt and with the air of a Carnegie parted with 8/6. I then went a walk with Jim and Ned. Wee Peg is now getting all right again.
Thursday Oct. 6	Heriot Watt in evening. The subject is Geofrey Chaucer, father of English poetry. Born about 1330. Died 1400. He wrote *The Canterbury Tales*.
Friday Oct. 7	"Sons" in evening. After the business we had a nice concert. Wee Peg is now alright again with the exception of a cough which troubles her a little at nights.
Saturday Oct. 8	This afternoon Liz, Peg and I went out. We saw a veteran's funeral. Another old soldier. The H.L.I. pipers played "The Flowers o' the Forest". In the evening I stayed in and watched wee Peg while Liz went out on some messages.
Sunday Oct. 9	For some time back, some stories of a disagreeable nature have been gossiped by some of my worthy relatives. Today I went to Sister Annie, then my mother, from both of whom I got a point blank denial. This in face of very strong proof. Later I went to G.'s. In the evening I went to class.

Monday Oct. 10	Public Library. Heriot Watt and then social meeting in Fountainbridge Church in evening. Some of the speeches were like a stormy night—windy! What a lot of mutual admiration! I wonder how people can sit and hear themselves praised in this manner. I am fond of praise myself but I would positively wither under yon idle flattery. This was at a P.S.A. meeting.
Tuesday Oct. 11	Tom McD. is off today. I asked Stoddart for a shift on to a cart. He'll see! I stayed in this evening and utilised my time with reading, writing and idling.
Wednesday Oct. 11	In the evening I attended open air socialist meeting at Murdoch Terrace. There was some good speaking done.
Thursday Oct. 13	Heriot Watt and then Guild in evening. Wee Peg is now much better.
Friday Oct. 14	Stayed indoors this evening. This is a change indeed. I am not on friendly terms with Miller. This is not a change.
Saturday Oct. 15	Today I again spoke to Stoddart re cart. I was unsuccessful but got the promise of the next. Now as the next opening may be in twenty years I will look foward with a mighty long look. We had a letter from Forbes'. They advise me to come to Canada.
Sunday Oct. 16	Our wee Peg is very fond of sweets and if she sees us with money, her hand is out and she keeps saying, "Feeties. Feeties." Yesterday I gave her a one pound note and she was strolling outside to buy "feeties". I reckon that would have done her for some time and we would have been living on "feeties" all the next week. What a sweet life it would be! Wee Peg is very bad with a cough. We went out in afternoon. I was along at G.'s and also Cairns'. Mick has now a phonograph. In the evening I visited Cousin Jean Forbes who is ill.
Monday Oct. 17	Heriot Watt in evening. I came right home from there.

Tuesday Oct. 18	There is a stir just now over my friends going about telling made-up stories about my wife. She, unable to bear it any longer, has put the matter in the hands of a writer. They, in the face of undeniable proofs deny all they have said. The lawyers say I need not pay my mother any aliment. Now I do not grudge her the little she gets from me, but I am not going to pay her and stand her abuse. Especially am I bound to do neither.
Wednesday Oct. 19	*Echoes* is out today. I have only a letter in. I was again indoors. We had several visitors whose talk was so bright that I nearly went to sleep in their company.
Thursday Oct. 20	G.'s and then Heriot Watt, after which I met Ned and Jim and had a walk.
Friday Oct. 21	This evening after taking the minutes of the Sons of Temperance meeting, I read my essay on Robert Fergusson, Scottish poet. It was well received.
Saturday Oct. 22	This afternoon I was met by my mother. I refused her her aliment until she apologises for those untruthful stories she has circulated. I afterwards went back to give her it but she was out.
	Liz and I later went up to the writer's. He again advised me not to give her anything. I stayed in in evening while Liz went out shopping.
Sunday Oct. 23	I was not outside until evening when Liz, Peg and I went to Aunt Forbes, Gorgie Road. Wee Peg was very ill during the night, her ears being the cause. They must have been very sore for although she was sound asleep, she was crying with the pain.
Monday Oct. 24	Today Wee Peg is much better. Her ears seem to have burst and given her relief. She has got another tooth.
	In the evening I was at Heriot Watt and library. I put in an exercise on Chaucer this evening. Needless to say, it is a masterpiece.
Tuesday Oct. 25	This evening I remained indoors to write an article for *Echoes* on Wm. Cobbett. I did not get it finished. That shows my diligence.

Wednesday Oct. 26	Liz and wee Peg were down at Cousin Jean's this evening. I went down for them. Later I attended meeting of the S.D.F. at Murdoch Terrace. An old man disturbed the meeting a good deal.
Thursday Oct. 27	Heriot Watt College in evening. Wee Peg is now thriving and speaking some. She has fairly mastered the baby language. Sometimes she talks away for a long time and nobody except perhaps another baby can understand her.
Friday Oct. 28	Stayed indoors and finished Cobbett.
Saturday Oct. 29	In the afternoon Liz and I went up and saw Mr. Balfour, writer, regarding a letter I received from a lawyer.
Sunday Oct. 30	This forenoon I went along to G.'s. Had walk with the 'boys'! In the afternoon I was at class when Miss R. gave a splendid lecture on St. Andrew, Scotland's Patron Saint. Miss R. is a genuine Christian!
Monday Nov. 1	This is an important day. This forenoon Liz went and saw the lawyer. In the afternoon I went and saw him and influenced a case that was seeming against me to my side. Today both the girls who have stayed with us for a long time were put away by Liz. This for keeping early morning hours. In the evening I was at Heriot Watt and then spree at G.'s. This is Hallowe'en. Tonight at G.'s I missed many dear faces but I see their double's in the rising generation.
Tuesday Nov. 2	Tonight I visisted a Son of Temperance home. I found that he has gone to S. Africa where he is doing well. It was a dirty day today.
Wednesday Nov. 3	This evening I went to the public library. Then to John Young's where I was introduced to a Scotch Comedian, Alex Glen. I was commissioned to write him some new Scotch comic songs.
Thursday Nov. 3	G.'s in the evening. Also Heriot Watt. Then Guild. This is the opening night. Mr D. S. Douglas read a paper "Character Studies from the Waverley Novels". It was most excellent good.

Monday Nov. 21	Tonight I had a visit from a comedian who asked me to write some songs for a pair. I had also a gentleman from the Liverpool Legal Friendly Society arranging with me to become a spare time agent. When he was gone I wrote a comic song for a pair.
Tuesday Nov. 22	This evening we were along at G.'s. It was bitter cold.

MY JOURNAL

William Anderson,

Year

1904:	Edinburgh, Review of Year
1905:	Edinburgh, Commencing January 22nd
1906:	Commencing June 9th to June 15th

Voyage to Canada, June 16th to June 26th on board Allan Lines Vessel "Sicilian"

Toronto, Canada, June 26th to June 30th

Taken from the diaries presently in the hands of Tom Coulston, grandson, Agincourt, Ontario.

As far as I know, these are the last diaries kept by my father, William Anderson.

Toronto, Ontario.
November 1982.   Olwen Anderson.

DIARY

The Year Just Gone—1904

The past year is in many respects a memorable one. Every year gives us some new experiences.

I have this year had a prose article inserted in *Echoes*; we have also lost some of our dearest friends; some have crossed the sea, others have crossed the bourne from whence no man returneth.

I have written an essay on Robert Fergusson which I have read to, and had well received at, St. Cuthbert's Guild and the Sons of Temperance.

I have joined the S.D.F., and other things which escape my memory for the time being have happened.

1905
Sunday
Jan. 22

Today we were along at G.'s, where I spent most of my spare time at the New Year, by the bye. In the afternoon Liz met Teen Berry and went with her to Mission Meeting. In the evening I went to S.D.F. meeting where Sinclair gave some of his experiences after twenty-three years in the Socialist movement. It was one of the most interesting lectures I ever listened to.

Monday
Jan. 23

This evening I was at the Heriot Watt College, then to library, then home where Mrs. Robertson, High Riggs, was waiting for me to write a letter for her.

Tuesday
Jan. 24

This evening, Mr. Gollogly and Mrs. Gollogly, junior, were along to our house for tea. We adjourned to their house. I went and brought Tom Robertson up with his gramophone and we had an enjoyable evening until nearly 11 p.m.

Wednesday Jan. 25	This is the day that "blast o' Januar win' blew hansel in on Robin". The blast is still blowing and has blown out the light of one of the finest young women I have ever known. A dear young soul of twenty-eight years has just succumbed to that murdering disease, pneumonia. She was kindly, goodhearted, and in fact, she was everything that was good—and now she is gone. Well, there are women whom we could better spare than Mrs. Smart. Dear Soul, may your rest be peaceful! I did not go out this evening.
Thursday Jan. 26	College this evening. The lesson was on Pope. I hurried home after. We generally have something to our cup of tea after our breakfast porridge. This morning it was salt fish. Wee Peg plunked her piece into her tea where it reclined for some minutes. It was then fished out and offered to me. With much politeness, I refused it. It was then handed to her mother who, not knowing where it had been, partook and did eat thereof.
Friday Jan. 27	Last evening coming home from Heriot Watt with a friend who is a bookseller's assistant, I was told that a swell, that is a half-nob will come in, purchase a book, take it away, read it, and return with it, saying that he intended giving it to a friend, but has found out that the friend already has the book; would the bookseller kindly give him a few that he may make his friend a present therefrom. He will retire with perhaps four and after reading the lot purchase one. He, of course, thinks the bookseller does not know he has read them all. But he does. No matter how cleaned the book is kept, he can tell.
	Annual Meeting of the "Sons" this evening.
Saturday Jan. 28	I went to two of the "Sons" today with their sick-money. This is a little apprenticeship as I was, last night, elected Sick Steward.
	In the evening Liz, Peg and I went down to my Aunt Jean's, then a walk along Dalry Road to G.'s, then to Robertson's in High Riggs. James is ill with bronchitis. We were home after 11 p.m.

St. Cuthbert's Church Young Men's Guild, *c.* 1903. William Anderson standing at extreme left.

Sunday Jan. 29	This morning I went down and saw Glen. Gave him a comic song and a waistcoat. Then I went to G.'s where I sold some tickets for a benefit concert for Sandie Glen. After that, Jim, John, Ned and his wife and I came along to our house for dinner.
	Another mean story of the middle class: A "gentleman" sent to a tailors for a fancy white vest. On the next morning, he returned it saying he did not want it now, would the tailor kindly take it back. But the tailor kindly refused as it had been worn overnight at a ball or something of the sort and bore marks of usage at the armpits.
Monday Jan. 30	This evening I was at Heriot Watt. The lesson was on Pope. Our teacher dwelt at some length on *The Dunciad*, a satirical poem in which he places all his literary enemies. Sir R. Bentley entitling himself to a prominent place for saying of Pope's *Iliad*, "A pretty story, Mr Pope, but you must not call it Homer."
	I met Ned outside and went home with him where we had a debate on religion. Jim argues from the evolution standpoint. He beat Ned on science and was told that he knew nothing.
Tuesday Jan. 31	Our wee Peg is a nice plain speaker. She takes this off her mother whose plain speaking to me is something painful. Of course, our wee girl has numerous good points; these she inherits from me. This evening, Liz and I went to G.'s and I had a walk with Jim and Ned.
Wednesday Feb. 1	The first month of 1905 has fled and here we are entered on the second month. By the bye, how is it that people don't wish you a Happy New Month after the same fashion as they wish us a Happy New Year; or a Happy New Week, or a Happy New Day for that matter? What happy times we would have. I was at Ned's at night. He came out with me as far as the Tron Church when I went to S.D.F. branch meeting.

Thursday Feb. 2	This is the Quarterly Rent day. Many poor souls are worrying over the raising of the wherewithal to pay that legal importer and drag on the people, the landlord. Our house was full of tranquil peace in the afternoon when Jim Gollogly came in and demanded me to make haste and come with him, John and Ned to the Empire. I made haste and neglected the Heriot Watt and Guild. The Empire was disappointing. There was a young lady, said to be only twelve years of age, who made a troupe of twelve lions go through a performance. What a taste we enlightened Britons have. We will flock in thousands to see some mortal risk their life or limb. I did not enjoy the young lady's performance but I liked seeing the lions. They were fine, clean brutes.
Friday Feb. 3	For some time I have not been feeling very well. Liz and I went along to G.'s. Ned, Jim and I had a walk. I could scarcely keep up with them, going only at a slow pace. We had to take a seat in Meadow Walk. Here I had a bygone evening recalled to me when once I sat with a former classmate of mine bearing the name of Miss Lizzie Lawson. She and I never were meant for one another, and I knew it. Yet she was a good lass, and I hope she gets a mate who is at least her equal. That is wishing her well.
Saturday Feb. 4	Today I still felt unwell. Liz, wee Peg and I were at G.'s in the afternoon. They went to the Grand Theatre in the evening. Liz and I went down the Canongate where we made some purchases then came along by Princes Street where I visited Dr. Stevens. He prescribed me a medicine which for horrible taste excels anything that ever crossed the threshold of my mouth.

Our wee Peg is thriving daily and like every other thriving child she has several nasty falls every day. Today she went bang against the dresser door with the result that she raised a howl and a lump on her forehead. This all comes in the way of thriving.

Sunday Feb. 5	This morning I was up at 7 a.m. I partook of a dose of my medicine. My previous opinion of it was confirmed. It is horrible stuff! I did not go out during the day. I wrote out part of my debate: "Is Drink the Cause of Poverty?" from a negative point. In the afternoon, Ned was along with wee Mick. We went out together. I left him at the end of Fountainbridge. I went and saw Jim Robertson. Then I went to S.D.F. meeting in "Son's" Hall. We held a business meeting.

Monday Feb. 6	Not feeling well this morning, I stayed in today and sent for the Dr. I was up for a short time during the day. In the afternoon I had a good sleep. Ned came along in the evening and Robertson came at 9.45 p.m. This evening, Mrs Kerr told us of a young woman who died and left a little girl of two years. The little girl, despite the fact that she was taken to a good home sobbed night and day for her mother until she, too, eventually died. This was very sad.

Tuesday Feb. 7	Today I don't feel so well as I felt yesterday. My back is sore and I can scarcely straighten myself. This is different from my usual. I being as a rule straightened. This afternoon, Dr. Stevens came and certified that I am suffering from a chill. Later Jim came along, then Ned. They both went away at 5:40 p.m. The rest of the evening was uneventful.

| Wednesday Feb. 8 | This is the first day I ever was in the Sheriff Court. Such a lot of lawyer busybodies. They put me in mind of a remark a visitor once let drop in a court room, "That's a bad looking lot you have here this morning, Sir." "Oh, these are not the prisoners, they are the lawyers." I was being sued by my mother for aliment. She was told to go to the Parochial Board and that they would try and find out my father. So in the meantime, the case is in my favour.

In the afternoon, Ned and I went to the funeral of Mr. Hutton, an old man of seventy years. Miller came in to see me. Afterwards Ned's wife was along. |
|---|---|

Thursday Feb. 9	This forenoon I went along to G.'s. Jim and I went for a walk. I called in at Mr. Porter's office and told his typewriter—Mr. P. being out—the results of the previous day's case at the court. Jim and I then came around by the High Street, Grassmarket and home. In the afternoon, Liz, wee Peg and I went to my Aunt in Gorgie Road. The evening was uneventful.
Friday Feb. 10	This forenoon I went along to old Mr. Sydney's and argued with him on social and religious subjects. In the afternoon we went along to G.'s. Home by 5 p.m. In bed shortly after 9 p.m. At 9:45 p.m. the "Gardener's" sick steward came with the money. This week we have had splendid weather, fine and dry but a little cold. I had a visit from Dr. MacDonald Robertson.
Saturday Feb. 11	This is another very fine day. I was in all the forenoon. At 1:00 p.m. I gave a run along to G.'s and hurried back to find that the Sick Steward had been and gone in my absence. I did not go out in the evening as the Templars' demand that their sick shall keep temperate hours—5 p.m.
Sunday Feb. 12	This is the first Sunday for a very long time that I have not been out. Ned came along for a couple of hours in the afternoon and a pretty uneventful Sunday found us in bed by about 9:15 p.m. By the bye, Dr. Stevens came in the afternoon and gave me another prescription.
Monday Feb. 13	This morning I went to Baildon's for medicine. I came through St. Cuthbert's Churchyard where I saw the grave of Thos. DeQuincey. This famous man expressed a desire that he may, when dead, be buried surrounded by rugged hills and here he lies with the Castle Rock in the near vicinity. I accompanied Ned on his rounds and called at the house of J. Campbell, 31 Carnegie Street with a pamphlet in the afternoon.
Tuesday Feb. 14	G.'s in the forenoon, also in afternoon. Jim is now ill, suffering from a severe pain in his side. I was home at 5:30 p.m. and wrote a letter to Dr. Kerr, City Hospital, re Maggie Jeffrey's clothing.

Wednesday Feb. 15	I was again at G.s today. Ned started writing out my paper on the negative side of "Is Drink the Cause of Poverty?" at my dictation, of course. The letter which I wrote to Dr. Kerr yesterday received a curt reply today. I was in bed early—about 9 p.m.
Thursday Feb. 16	Again at G.s. Jim is still in bed but not very ill. In the afternoon Liz, wee Peg and I went to Mrs. Strachan's, Carnegie Street. We took the bus from the South side and were home by 6 p.m. No visitors. I was again in bed by about 9 p.m.
Friday Feb. 17	I went along to G.s in afternoon. It was cold and drizzly. I went with Ned to Duke Street. In the evening when at home, I wrote the finish to my debate. I was really thankful to see the last word of it written. I heaved a sigh of relief and then went to bed. Time 10 p.m. This forenoon I wrote a letter to Sir Henry Littlejohn for Mrs. Jeffrey.
Saturday Feb. 18	This morning I was out at 9:10 a.m. I went to Dr. Stevens then to Stoddart's then to G.'s and from there to prospective landlord, then again to Dr. Stevens. After that I met and had nearly an hour's talk with Davie Ovenstone, then to chemist's, then Tom Robertson's and home. Mrs. Jeffrey came down with a nice reply she had got from Sir H. Littlejohn in answer to my letter of yesterday. In the evening, I had Tom Robertson up to G.'s with his gramophone. We had an enjoyable time. This was another miserable day—full of blizzards.
Sunday Feb. 19	It is cold this morning. There are intervals of sun and showers but there is one continuous storm at our house. I went along to Hadden's until the storm blew by. When I came back, comparative calm had been restored. Last night a girl came to stay with us for a week or so. This forenoon I went along to G.'s, had a walk with Jim and Ned. I got home at 5 p.m. and was kept indoors for the rest of the evening.

Monday Feb. 20	This morning I resumed my beloved employment of coal carrying. What a glorious vocation and what a prospect—climbing stairs forever until laid aside in premature age and then after a life of industry. Oh, Horror! The working man's retiring mansion—the grubber, or in refined English, the workhouse. In the evening, I went to Heriot Watt, called at Jim Robertson's and then home. Mrs. R. was at our house, also Jean Forbes.
Tuesday Feb. 21	Today I spoke to Allan & Stoddart about the house at West Kilbride for Jas. Robertson. In the evening, Liz, wee Peg and I called on Robertson and then to G.'s. Jim is busy painting. He showed me a picture which he said was the sea. I thought it was the sky upside down. Jim is a good drawer for all that, and I have commissioned him to draw me two masterpieces for nothing. Talk about exploiting talent—I'm there every time.
Wednesday Feb. 22	Today I wrote a letter to Mr. Wallace for Jas. Robertson. In the evening I went along to Robertson, then to S.D.F. meeting where I took the chair. Home at 10:45 p.m. Ned and Maggie had just gone from our house.
Thursday Feb. 23	This evening I went to G.s, then to Heriot Watt, then to Gunn's. Coming home at 10:30 p.m., an organ grinder turned up a close in the Cowgate with his organ. A boy shouted to a companion, "Oh, look at the organ. It's time ye were on top of it with a wee chain round your neck." This is not a new joke but it was the smart way in which it was said that tickled me.
Friday Feb. 24	This is an important evening. I have to read a paper on the negative side of the question "Is Drink the Cause of Poverty?" I have read my paper on the above question. It was well received. As the hour was late, discussion was not allowed and so something was lost. I believe that on a show of hands I would have won the debate.
Saturday Feb. 25	G.'s in afternoon and again in evening as Jim is still on the sick list. He could not get out of bed.
	After tea, Liz, wee Peg & I went to G.'s. We did not go out during the evening.

Sunday Feb. 26	After dilly-dallying during the fore part of the day, I went along to G.'s in time to meet the boys coming in from a walk. I had dinner with the G.'s and was home at 5 p.m. Did not go out in evening.
Monday Feb. 27	Heriot Watt in evening. After that to G.'s. I had a visit of Glen, Scotch Comedian. His benefit is not promising well. That is a pity. The Templars true to their custom and untrue to their promises have failed to reply to his benefit. Ned and Maggie were along.
Tuesday Feb. 28	The second month gone. What a whizzing month ours is to be sure. There are two months gone already. The girl who has been staying with us leaves this evening. She is a servant and starts in a "place" this evening. Tonight I was at G.'s when we had a talk over religion and history. Today, I started a subscription list for Jas. Robertson who is now on his sixth week of illness. I was fairly successful. One man told me he is not such a fool as to give anything towards Jim. What a good thing it is that all the men are not wise in that sense.
Wednesday March 1	Tonight I have a meeting to attend. Liz wanted me to come out with her. Of course, her majesty woman had to be obliged and like a lamb I went with her to G.'s. And the business of the world is at a standstill because I cannot get to that meeting. We had great laughs at the antics of wee Peg in G.'s.
Thursday March 2	Tonight I came from Heriot Watt to the Guild. We had a splendid essay on Sir Walter Scott from Wm. Grieve. I said a few words and came away early. Mrs. Robertson was in. Jim had got a notice from West Kilbride to come to the home for a fortnight. He was to leave the next day, March 3rd.
Friday March 3	This evening I went over to Strachan's, then to Parker's where I got the money for the sick. We came along to G.'s, Liz and I, when I paid Jim his one pound. I am Sick Steward for the "Sons".

Saturday March 4	Today I was busy taking in the contributions to the subscription. I have 22/- and 5/- to come yet. The list has to go round the other stations. After dinner, I started on my round of sick visits. I started at Merchiston Mews, then to Gorgie, Bothwell Street, Arthur Street and Sciennes. It was a hard afternoon's work as I had wee Peggy with me. One of the sick is suffering from melancholia. In the evening, Jim and Ned and I had a walk.
Sunday March 5	In the afternoon I was with Liz and wee Peg to the christening party of Mr. and Mrs. McIntosh's baby. In the evening, I was at Socialist Meeting at E. Register Street. Sinclair Morton and Gunn were the speakers. I was home at 10:00 p.m.
Monday March 6	Today I sent lists for Jim Robertson's subscription to the other stations. I have received 6/- from the office. This evening I was with Liz to a sale in Lothian Street. I was not five minutes there when I had to come out with wee Peg. We went to G.'s later. I made a resolution to be in bed early tonight. I got there after 11 p.m.
Tuesday March 7	This was Sandie Glen's (Scotch Comedian) Benefit Night. It was held in Oddfellows Hall and was a huge success. It was crowded. I sat and listened to the people laughing at the songs and would-be jokes that I wrote for Sandie. A comedian had me ushered into his mighty presence and gave me orders to write comic songs for him at nothing each. I reminded him that I could get plenty customers of his kind. We took the bus home.
Wednesday March 8	This evening Glen was along and gave me 10 shillings as part-payment for songs written. I would not have written as many to anybody for that amount but Sandie is a nice chap and I am glad I obliged him. Liz got the 10 bob. I wrote the songs. Liz got the cash and there you are. We were at G.'s later.

Thursday March 9	This evening I was at Heriot Watt. I came away earlier and found Ned and Maggie awaiting me at our house. We had a pleasant evening and suppered on tea and new pancakes. We are leaving our house here and are looking after one in 49 Fountain Bridge. I think I will get it. The Rent is £9.15.0.
Friday March 10	Tonight Ned was at the Empire and I had to go to the "Sons" meeting alone. I spoke on the Dr.'s case. He is very careless and I pointed out an instance to the members. It has to be enquired into. Last night I called on Tom Dickson. I saw him in the throes of death. He died this morning at 12:30 a.m.
Saturday March 11	This was a dirty drizzly day. I sallied forth to pay the sick. I trudged down to Gorgie Road, then to Bothwell Street. Then to Arthur Street, and finished up in Sciennes. It was a terrible afternoon and I would rather have been at home quarrelling with the wife. There's a happy ideal for you. . . This afternoon I gazed for the last time on the dead face of Thomas A. Dickson, a member of our Sunday Class. He was a nice lad, age 21 years, and I am sorry to see him lying there. I am more sorry for his parents who will sadly miss their dear son. God grant you rest, Tommy.
Sunday March 12	This morning I wrote a letter to Jim Robertson who is now on his second week at the Cooperative Homes, West Kilbride. I went along to G.'s at 12 noon. P. Welsh and Frank are home for a week-end from Otterburn. Ned, Jim, John and I had a walk. I was home about 2 p.m. In the evening Liz and I went along again. We had another walk while Liz stayed in G.'s. We were home about 10 p.m.

I was at the class this afternoon. Miss Robertson paid a tribute to our late classmate, T. A. Dickson. She stopped for a second or two at intervals and I could see that she was very much affected. She is a kindly lady and a good Christian to boot.

Monday March 13	For the first time for very many months I attempted serious verse. It was on T. A. Dickson. I feel the loss of this good young lad who died on Friday last.
	This evening I had a walk with Liz and then took Peg home while her Mother was at a sale. My cousin, Jean Forbes, came up. Maggie Tucker's breast is very sore and Liz took her up to the Dr. Like a good Dr. he was out when most needed.
	This morning I sent a letter to Jas. Robertson, West Kilbride.
Tuesday March 14	This morning I had a letter from J. R. I wrote out some verses on the death of Tom Dickson. I took them up to Miss Robertson who said they were all right. Hadden also said that. I then went with Ned to the Entertainment Committee Meeting of the "Sons" where we made some of the final arrangements for our coming great concert in the Central Halls. I have to act as steward. Hope I am taking money. The tickets are selling well.
Wednesday March 15	This was a very blowy day. Chimney cans are over all of the streets. Two horses have been killed and many plate glass windows broken. I intended going to the S.D.F. meeting but fate and the wife ruled otherwise and I found myself along at G.'s. Ned started making a book yesterday. These two days have been successful. We have got settled about another house in 49 Fountainbridge. Rent £9.9.0. 3 Places.
Thursday March 16	This evening I was at Heriot Watt and then the Guild. We had a splended essay from the Rev. Mr. Fulton on John Brown, M.D., author of *Rab and His Friends*. I enjoyed it very well and said a few words on it. There were only about eleven present. I had a bigger audience than that myself for my essay on Robert Fergusson, Poet. I must be the better essay-writer of the two—the reverend gentleman and I.

Friday March 17	This evening I had as usual several different places to go to not being able to go to them all. At once I went to the "Sons" Executive Meeting and discussed with them re the disposal of tickets for the entertainment to be held in Central Halls on March 31st. I got the names of several members to call on. After that I got the sick money from the secretary and modestly withdrew.
Saturday March 18	What a splendid day this is! I sallied forth in the afternoon to pay my respects and their money to the sick and wounded of the Order of the Sons of Temperance. After a walk beginning in Sciennes, Beaumont Place, Dalgety Avenue and Bothwell Street, I finished in Gorgie. I then went up to my Aunt's where I met my wife and wee Peg. I had a look from my Aunt's window at the Hearts v. Airdrieonians football match. We were at G.'s at night.
Sunday March 19	This finishes Jas. Robertson's first week at the Home at West Kilbride. I am busy taking up a subscription for him. What a lot of rudeness one has to put up with when gathering in money from working men. I went up to G.'s and had a walk with them. Class in afternoon. I took wee Peg along Princes Street in evening.
Monday March 20	This evening I went up to Mrs. Robertson and gave her 30/- subscription money. My suggestion to send 5/- to James was met with a violent negative. It was thus postponed. After Heriot Watt I went to G.'s.
Tuesday March 21	This morning I got 6/- from the office on behalf of the subscription fund. I sent it on to Jas. R.
Wednesday March 22	I was at the S.D.F. meeting this evening. A Spaniard who has been a teacher of languages at Heriot Watt became a member. He told some interesting stories of Socialism in Spain.
Thursday March 23	This has been a horrible day since the afternoon. It has poured rain incessantly. I intended going to Heriot Watt and then Guild. I never got any further than the fireside. One wetting in one day is at least sufficient for me. And thus it was that the wife got the benefit of my genial society.

Friday March 24	This evening I did some visiting on behalf of the "Sons" with concert tickets. I then went to the meeting. I got the sick money from Parker and was home about 11 p.m.
Saturday March 25	This was another miserable afternoon. I sallied forth to pay the sick money to the unwell members. I wonder if I would be expelled if they knew that I got a wet. Fancy getting a wet while at Temperance work. As a rule it is a dry job. Jim Robertson was along this forenoon and put tackets and two plates in my boots. I stayed in at night while Liz was out.
Sunday March 26	Walk with the boys this forenoon. Sleep in afternoon, then G.'s at night when I had another walk with the boys. Frank is home with a sore hand.
Monday March 27	This morning, Jim Robertson started his work again. This evening, I wrote letters to *Echoes* and Mr. Wallace for Jim. I then went to Heriot Watt and G.'s.
Tuesday March 28	Today is the first big race day in the G.'s book. Lincoln Handicap. Every horse was favourite. Strange to say only one did win. Now according to the tipsters every one should have been first. I was along this evening and had a walk with Jim and Ned. Ned came along to our house for his wife but she was gone.
Wednesday March 29	This evening I met Ned and went with him to Entertainment Meeting of the Sons at 142 High Street. Home at 10:45 p.m.
Thursday March 30	This evening we had our last lecture for the season. It was on Goldsmith and was splendid. I came from Heriot Watt to Glen St. Hall where there was an excursion meeting of the employees. I was nominated for committee but just my luck, I was out of it on the vote.

Friday March 31	This finishes the third month of the year. The first quarter is gone. Tonight the first concert of the Sons of Temperance was held in Central Halls. There was one specially good item by Miss Marie Thom, "Dark Lochnagar". It was magnificent! I never mind of hearing a song better rendered. Thanks, Miss Thom. After the concert, the workers of the various divisions of the "Sons" met and had tea and a talk with Bro. Gleadhill from Hull. With 75,000 less people in Hull than in Edinburgh, they have over 11,000 "Sons". We in Edinburgh only number 800. Bro. G. blames lack of enterprise and push among the workers for the small number.
Saturday April 1	This is all fools' day. As showing how this day's silly tricks—known as practical jokes—are dying out, I never heard of one instance today. This is all a tendency of the times. We are a serious people and haven't time to joke. Joke! poor souls, we can scarcely find food far less jokes. This afternoon I went to the Lyceum Theatre and saw F. R. Benson & Coy. play *Hamlet*. It was a splendid performance. The theatre differs from the outside world for this reason, that they give a very high position to the poor. Oh, ye Gods, at a tanner a time! This is the reward of your industry.
Sunday April 2	This morning, as usual, I was up and doing nothing. At 12:40 p.m., my Aunt Jean came in, and I along with little Peg went with her to the cemetery. There are some people delight in walking through cemeteries. I met a man and wife there who after exhausting themselves there were going to Warriston Cemetery. "What," asked I. "Going to Warriston?" "Yes," said the man, "We go round the cemeteries every Sunday. Last Sunday we were at Echobank." This setting out from Gorgie Road would surely serve any cemetery appetite. I went to class at 5 p.m. Then G.'s in evening.

Monday April 3	Some time ago, our teacher at Heriot Watt announced a Poetry Competition. The theme to be "The First Snowdrop". I handed in my effort tonight. This is the examination evening. We got five questions out of which we had to answer four. I answered:

Give the rise of the English novel;

What was the train of thought occupied by Gray in his Elegy;

Give reasons for the popularity of the Elegy;

Give an account of Goldsmith's Continental Tour; and

Why does Gibbon occupy such a high place in History?

Each of these questions is beyond me, but I am a chap with a big heart, and I made the effort. If I don't get the prize medal there will be an injustice done. G.'s later. Walk with Ned and Jim.

Tuesday
April 4

All great men keep a diary. Hence this. Many hundreds of years after this when an interested British Race are reading these entries they will exclaim, "Good Heavens! What a genius! Why didn't they shoot him?"

This evening I did not feel well and went down to Dr. Stevens from whom I got a prescription. I went to Baildon's and was told to come back in half an hour. I said I could not, but that I would sit and wait on it, and my obnoxious presence in the shop made them serve me in a hurry I can assure you. When any "Lady" came in covered with cheap fur, they did not tell her to come back in half an hour. Like the sycophants they are, they were running into each other to serve her. No class war. Ahem!

Wednesday
April 5

Today I still felt unwell and did not go out to work. At 9 a.m., I went down to the Dr.'s but he was not up out of bed. And he was not up, he was not down. He sleeps upstairs, you see. I went up to G.'s and accompanied Ned to the General P.O., then the Revenue Office. There stood a big chap at the Revenue Office door ready to ask what our business was. We treated him with contempt and like people who knew our own business there, though I did not, we walked past him as if he were a statue. In the afternoon, I went to bed where I was out of everybody's way and slept for about three hours. Mine's is a sleeping trouble. I think it is chronic as I am always sleepy.

114

Thursday April 6	I said my disease is a sleepy one. Some time ago while listening to a lecture I was doing my best to look interested and yet overcome with sleep. I imagined the paper on the wall to be so many phantoms and then I thought I saw a lady just about to fall, and with commendable gallantry I was about to spring across the floor to catch her when I awoke. What a good job I did not make that spring!

Today the Store coalmen sat for their photo. It is as well for the group that I was not present. Still there are uglier persons than me going the rounds; and, poor weak things, they think they are good looking. This morning I went down and saw Dr. Stevens. In the afternoon, I saw Dr. Robertson. Got sick line from each. I went down to my Aunt's in Gorgie Road at 4:15 p.m. In the evening I went to Heriot Watt. Here our class got the job to write an essay on Goldsmith's *Deserted Village*. Later, I attended business meeting of the Guild where I was again made assistant librarian. I came home from there nearly dead with a pain in the region of the third button of the waistcoat.

Friday April 7th	Today I did not go out until the afternoon when I went with Liz and wee Peg to Strachan's. I was home with wee Peg at 7:15 p.m. John King came along and sat for some time after which I went to bed. Liz came home about 10 p.m.

Saturday April 8	Today I feel a lot better. I lay in bed until 12 noon. Tom came in afternoon with my wages—8/- for two days. Then came the "Gardeners' man" with 8/4 less 2/6—5/10. The "Sons" man did not come today. What can be wrong? are the "Sons" broke? I met Stoddart this evening. He was more concerned about when I would resume work than my general health. Oh, he is a genuine Christian! What a love he has for his fellowman. What a following out of the teachings of Christ! But I'll say no more.

Sunday April 9	This morning accompanied by wee Peg I paid Hadden a state visit. Later I called on the G.'s and had a walk with Ned and John. Ned stood milk; John stood cigarettes, and I partook thereof. In the afternoon Ned, Jim and Frank came along and had tea at our house. Frank was suffering with pains in his head. He has a touch of blood poisoning at present. For myself, I feel much better today. I did not go out this evening.
Monday April 10	Today were I a man of means—instead of which I am a mean man—I would call all my friends together, kill the fatted calf, have the flowing goblet brought hence and hold high festival. Cos why? Well, because I have won the poetry competition at the class in Heriot Watt College. My prize is two volumes *Choice Essays* and *Virgil's Works* translated by John Dryden. Both very fine books and I am mighty proud of them. Oh, there is no doubt about it, I am a 'grate Poit'. I wrote to Forbes, Canada, and Miss Robertson, Cork, today. We had a walk along Princes Street, Liz, wee Peg and I.
Tuesday April 11	Today I went along to G.'s. I showed Jim my prize. He was pleased to learn that I had won the competition. I had wee Peg with me. She went to sleep in G.'s. After she awoke, we both came home for dinner. In the afternoon, I finished Bax's *History of the French Revolution*. It is a nice little book and I believe very accurate. In the evening, I went up and saw Mr. John Grant about an overcharge of 1/3 against me in the Free Gardeners. I then finished the evening at home over my books. I feel the pain again this evening. Last night I fared badly with my exam paper only gaining 16 marks out of, I think, a possible 100. For an essay on *The Deserted Village*, I took 50 out of a possible 100—a little better!
Wednesday April 12	Well, here I am at 2:40 p.m. in the day and am not cleaned yet. Liz is out at a sale and I am here in charge of our family of one, wee Peg. In the afternoon, I washed myself—what a change—and went along to G.'s.

Liz was again at the sale this evening. She came home in triumph bearing a child's coat and hat as trophies. A woman's first desire is to have a baby; her second is to have it well dressed. It is well-dressed if it has better clothing on than her neighbour's children.

Thursday April 13	Today my wife has still got that attack of sale fever. I'm sure she'll buy a bargain yet. Ha, I thought so. Here she comes with several (9) balls of crochet cotton and a white silk muffler. Total cost 2/5. In the afternoon I went up and saw Dr. Robertson. Mrs Strachan visited us this afternoon. Liz and she indulged in small talk. I retired to my private sitting room and read part of Goldsmith's *She Stoops to Conquer*. It is very funny. I should have been at the Guild this evening. Today I bought Peg a sugar-man. Female-like, she began to worry him. He did not keep his head long. He was indeed too sugary at first.
Friday April 14	One day this week, we bought Peggy a painted ball. She immediately showed her appreciation of our gift by chewing half the paint off it! And in the first few minutes.

This evening I visited Dr. Stevens. In the afternoon, I also saw Dr. Robertson. It was a wild night. I called in at Mr. Grieve's our last year's Guild President. Bro. Wiseman came tonight with the "Son's" money. |
Saturday April 15	This morning I had a good walk round the bookshops after seeing Stoddart and telling him of my intention to resume work next week. I purchased one book at a penny, and a hundred envelopes at 2d., total 3d. There was a mistake in my money from the "Gardeners". I went up to Bro. Grant and had it made right by coming away with another 2/-. In the evening, I had a walk with the G's.
Sunday April 16	There is no knowing where one's footsteps will take him. This forenoon Ned and I had a walk together and found ourselves in the Dean Cemetery. Here we saw the grave of Sir Hector MacDonald. I was at the class at 5 p.m., and my Aunt Jean's at Gorgie at 7 p.m. with Liz and wee Peg.
Monday April 17	This is Spring holiday. The poet who would dare to sing the beauties of Spring on a day such as this ought to be drawn and quartered. I was along at G.'s in the forenoon. In the afternoon, I wrote a short article on Goldsmith's *Deserted Village*. I took car with the G.'s for Portobello at 4 p.m. It was bitter cold and we were home at 7:20 p.m.

Tuesday April 18	Today, though not feeling very well, I resumed my work. It is such a nice light job that one need scarcely stay off, even though half dead. It is a charming occupation is coal carrying. In the evening, I saw Dr. Robertson and got a prescription. Some time ago, I awarded the palm to Dr. Stevenson for the bitterest medicine that was ever prescribed by mortal man. I withdraw the prize and now present it to Dr. Robertson. His will be hard to beat.
Wednesday April 19	This evening I did not feel very well. I stayed indoors to recruit. I wrote an article entitled "A Walk Through Dean Cemetery". Liz is away spreading our superfluous wealth at an auction sale. Some women are sale-mad. But where there is baby clothes for sale, my wife is sale-frantic!
Thursday April 20	This evening I saw Dr. Stevens. He put me off the sick list. I then went to Guild where there was a committee meeting being held to arrange next session's syllabus. Two of the essays are "Macbeth", and "The French Revolution". I went up the road a bit with Mr. Cairns, and gave my articles on Goldsmith and the "Dean Cemetery".
Friday April 21	This evening I was again feeling unwell. I went along to G.'s and then went with Ned to "Sons" meeting. There was a lot of business and it was 10:20 p.m. when we came out. I heard 12 o'clock strike. A nice hour for a sick man to be lying awake especially when he must be up at shortly after 5 a.m.
Saturday April 22	All this week the weather has been bitter cold and if it were not for the calendar I would not think it is Spring. It is still cold. I had my articles through the post from Mr. Cairns this morning. He suggests that I should turn my "Cemetery" article into verse as the reflections are hardly suitable for a prose article.

Sunday April 23	This is Easter Sunday. Last night I was seized with a fit of generosity and bought a half dozen eggs at 4½d. Today I had a walk with the G.'s at 3 p.m. I went to Panmure Place and saw the funeral of my late schoolmaster, Mr. Patrick Corbett. He was something like forty years in the Vennel School. His career has been a most useful one. In the afternoon I was at the class, then to Mr. Andrews' with whom I walked along Princes Street. I met the G.'s later and had a walk with them. I did not feel well.
Monday April 24	I have a p.c. for a meeting tonight. Didn't go. Not well. Wrote to Mrs. Cockburn, America.
Tuesday April 25	Still feeling unwell. I have a lot of writing to do but at present am quite unable to tackle it.
Wednesday April 26	This morning our under-foreman, R. Freer, a little under the influence of drink, quarrelled with one of the men and got himself dismissed. He deserves this, yet it is a pity. This evening, I felt at the worst stage as yet of my illness and yet I wrote out lines on "Our Trip to Ayr" and sent them to *Echoes*. In bed at 8 p.m.
Thursday April 27	This morning I felt a deal better after a good night's rest. Throughout the day I felt better. I wrote out the article on *The Deserted Village* tonight. Later, I felt as bad as ever. This pain is terrible. I can scarcely bear it.
Friday April 28	Today I felt a deal better and while up at High Riggs biscuit factory, I ate biscuits and oatcakes and drank some milk with impunity. My book case is now full. It has cost me many an ill-spared 6d. to do this, and yet there are many I could give away and not miss. For all that, there are many working men who would not cast out with my humble library. Prominent on the top shelf stands the bold Shakespeare. Not far from him we have our human bard, Burns. Thomson, Shelley, Pope, Longfellow and Josephus are all represented. The author who ranks with these is in good company.

119

Saturday April 29	This afternoon we had a visit from Miss MacLaren, schoolteacher, Inverleithen. Later I wrote out and sent to *Echoes* editor, "Thoughts on Goldsmith's *Deserted Village* and "In Dean Cemetery". It rained very heavily. In the evening, Liz and I went to G.'s. Liz took wee Peg home. Jim and Johnny and I went a walk. Ned was at Glasgow for the "Sons". We met him in Princes Street at 10:40 p.m. I was home at 11:30 p.m. I have felt alright today and am thankful.
Sunday April 30	This morning I again feel well. At 12:20 p.m. I went along to Ned's. Had walk with the boys. In the afternoon, my Aunt Jean and her daughter, Peggy, called in. I was in at Hadden's today. He told me of a poem he once wrote. His father suggested numerous alterations. Hadden sent it with alterations and also in the original state to *People's Journal*. The original was accepted and old Hadden gave up criticising for a time. King's in evening. Then a walk. Did not feel well again this evening.
Monday May 1	Hurrah! Summer has come. This is according to the calendar, but not according to the weather. This evening, Ned, Jim and Johnny G., and John Rafferty and I did the tanner stalls of the Lyceum where we were much amused by the musical comedy "Sergeant Brue". The old Sergeant Brue has been left a lot of money which he has only to receive on his becoming inspector. The dodges adopted to get him promoted are very funny. A burglary is planned. Sergeant Brue is lying under the bed in wait. The burglars, however, shirk the job and according to plan, the police are called in and Sergeant Brue hauled out from under the bed and charged with burglary.
Tuesday May 2	This is my thirtieth birthday. The tens are interesting stages in our career, and this is my third time. Well, I am getting on. I am getting full of years. My house is full of presents, amounting in all to a pair of socks from Liz. Still I am jolly pleased. Many a man is dead before he is thirty—there's consolation for a suffering soul. After all, people who are dead are not badly off. Liz was at my Aunt Jean's, Gorgie. I went down for her: after that I went to G.'s. It was a wet night. The weather clerk generally celebrates my birthday with a shower. I think it is to drown my luck.

Wednesday May 3	I feel a great deal better tonight. I went with Jim Nugent to learn him to cycle. He rode very well, both mounting and dismounting with ease. I also had a spin. His is a free wheel cycle and I felt awkward on it, with the result that I got confused on it and made a frantic effort to force the top of my head through a thick stone wall. I think the head got the worst of that deal. While Nugent was riding up and down I wrote a poem about a man who lost his head and heart through seeing a lovely young lady. It rained heavily. I was home at 7:40 p.m. & in bed at 9:20 p.m.
Thursday May 4	Today I heard of the death of old Mrs. Davidson, Newburgh. Well, this is another of the old school away. We don't raise women of her kidney nowadays. She was a good old soul and I am sorry I did not look on her cheery old face in life again before she died. Were I to go back to Newburgh, it would not seem the same place. Well, well, Granny, may your bones rest in peace and your soul soar to Heaven, there to intermingle with kindred good souls. I was at G.'s in evening and Guild later. Went home with Mr. Cairns, and was home at 11:30 p.m.
Friday May 5	Today I sent a letter of sympathy to Mr. and Mrs. Beckit, Newburgh, on their Mother's death. Ned's Mother and his wife went through there this morning. I got a p.c. from Ned's wife. I should have liked to have gone through to pay my last respects but economic pressure denied me that privilege. In the afternoon, I went to Mrs. Veitch's, Downfield Place, for Liz and wee Peg. Mrs. V. has been very ill but is now recovering. And now I expect Auld Granny Davidson is in her grave. Her old bones are laid in their last resting place and years will come and go and she no change will know. And thus it is whole populations pass away.
Saturday May 6	This afternoon I took wee Peg with me on my sick visits for the "Sons". I started at Dundee Place, then to Keir Street, then to Sciennes, then to Montague Street, then to Grindlay Street where I drew our dividend from the Store, then home. Not a bad carry for a little girl of two years. In the evening I carried her about another two miles and was called lazy for complaining. 'Tis an awful world this! I was tired and went to bed early, viz., 10 p.m.

I

Sunday May 7	This morning I was up shortly after 7 a.m. It was a lovely morning and bids fair to be the opening of summer proper. This forenoon, I was along at G.'s. In the afternoon, I was at class. I went from there to Grant's, Lady Lawson Street, and accompanied him to the S.D.F. rooms. There was no out-door meeting as both Gunn and Leslie are unwell. Gunn who is a man well-versed in many subjects told us some things about cloth manufacture and flaws in cloth.
Monday May 8	There are several kinds of fever which the feminine body is subject to. One is the spring-cleaning fever; another is the moving-cleaning. Woe to the man that comes near a women when attacked by the former. My wife at present has a bad attack of the latter, and our articles of furniture are in a deevil o' a steer. I am confined to the house to make myself useful! Godelpus! Fancy me being useful.
Tuesday May 9	My wife is still suffering from that dreadful complaint known as removal fever. Today at 9 a.m. I went along and started in the furniture department for a day. Miller and I were away round by Granton and Leith after doing Stockbridge. We were constant on the road from 9 a.m. till 8.30 p.m. It was a long spell and I was sick of it. Ned's wife and Barbara were along.
Wednesday May 10	I intended going to a meeting tonight but fate and my wife have ruled otherwise, and I have to accompany her to G.'s. Although the house that Mrs. Leadbetter is removing to is empty, she will not flit. Were she to do so, we would lose no time in occupying the house she vacates. I am tired of 105 Dundee Street. The weather just now is excellent. It is, of course, too warm for coal carrying but it doesn't matter about us.
Thursday May 11	Tonight instead of going to the Guild I stayed at home and made myself 'useful'. That is, I looked on while Liz did all the work. It is often the case that the person doing least gets most credit. A fortnight ago I sent two prose articles and a piece of verse on our forthcoming trip to *Echoes*. I enclosed a stamped envelope for return if unsuitable. They are not back yet, which is a good sign. I am a 'grate writer'.

Friday May 12	This evening I strolled leisurely over to Parker's, taking looks over the books at the various bookstalls on the way. Any person would have thought to have seen me that I was on the verge of buying a pound's worth right there. But nay. When I got the sick money from Parker and with the air of a benefactor I went around and paid the sick. I was at home at 9:20 p.m.
Saturday May 13	This afternoon there was a great demonstation of the Trades to protest against the rejection of the Trades Dispute Bill. Thousands turned out to witness the procession but only hundreds listened to the speeches which were of a high order. I visited the Strachans, then Parkers, then home, on my way from the King's Park where the demonstration took place. Later Liz and wee Peg and I had a walk and met the G.'s boys. This has been a nice day.
Sunday May 14	Last evening I promised Ned I would come along for him at 6 a.m. this morning but who pays any attention to a promise made on Saturday nights? Ned came along for me at nearly 12 p.m. and I was in bed. I got up, dressed and we went round by Corstorphine. In the evening, I went to S.D.F. meeting at E. Register Street. I had wee Peg with me.
Monday May 15	I thought to have flitted to our new house this evening, but the good lady of the other refuses to move, hence our delay. Her name is Leadbetter. I wish she had been lead-better when she was young. We are daily expecting an interesting event to take place in our happy home. This will enable me to refer to my family in a plural sense. Wae's me! and wae's my wife!
Tuesday May 16	Here we are, still at 105, and everything is in a stir. I can't move for bales of floorcloth and chairs and tables all mixed together, and my wife is sublimely happy for a woman dearly loves to mix things up a deal. I have heard that the woman whose house we are about to enter is a very nice woman. She may be but in the face of a lot of evidence to prove it, I'd still doubt it. This because she won't flit.

123

Wednesday May 17	There are five tenants living in the back land at 105 Dundee Street. We are all flitting. This breaks up some friendships as we are all on good terms with each other. So friendly in fact, that we could borrow money from each other. There's friendship for you! I am still busy packing everything into boxes and baskets. What a terrible mix-up there is. My books are tied into bundles and put into two bags. They are very heavy. Of course, learning is a heavy matter. Besides, my books contain some solid matter.
Thursday May 18	Thursday is our Guild night but behold I am not there. I would that I could escape all this terrible stir and flee down to the Guild, there to intermix and talk with the intellectuals of St. Cuthbert's. But no, fate and a stern wife rule otherwise and here I am still busy packing. The things seem to be multiplying. When I was a kid I used to think flitting a grand thing, now my mind has violently changed on that score.
Friday May 19	Tonight I am out for a breath of fresh air and to go to the meeting of the Sons of Temperance. We had a good meeting. Several members stayed behind to take their degrees. I don't approve of the Degree Temple as it is making an unnecessary circle, and goodness knows, as a Friendly Society, we are unfriendly enough without making sections.
Thursday May 23	Tonight we removed to our new domicile. As usual, there is the usual fault-finding with my work. This proves me to be a successful man. We got the beds up and then offered up thanks!

Wednesday June 7	The rest of the time has been utilised in putting things to right, and now I find myself on June 7th the father of a little boy. A dear little chap who turned the scale—a thing not much thicker than a pencil, by the way—at seven pounds. He seemed to frown. Perhaps he was angry at having to come into this world where millions of dear children are starving.
	Can you wonder that I walk with an elastic lightness. I believe I could win the walking championship just now. I would be a light weight. I am so light-hearted. The wee boy is getting on fine but still frowning as if not yet reconciled. Liz is also doing well for which I am glad. Ned's wife is in attendance. When the Doctor broke the news to me that it was a boy, I ate my kipper as if it were a beefsteak. And then I went on my way to my work rejoicing. This was 9 a.m. I sent p.c. to Strachan: "Unto us a son is born. Both doing well. And I am as well as can be expected."
Thursday June 8	There is a young man, aged eighteen years, has just died in the stair next to ours. His death was caused through taking an ice-cream drink. This is most pitiful. There is also the death of a friend in Leith and a friend just opposite, and a girl up our stair gets married tonight and we have a baby born. And so the world goes on— marriages, births and deaths. What a world! Truly the unseen Power is the greatest Power on earth. I had a walk with Ned and Jim and P. Welsh. The latter was up this evening and gave us three nice photos.

There is an old custom when a baby is born to slip a coin into its hand when seen by visitors. This is a good custom. It is not so good when I visit a new baby. My grandfather when each of his grandchildren was born used to slip a half-sovereign into the little creature's palm. When I came on the scene, he, as a result of overjoy or overdrink, slipped a second one into my hand. This pointed out luck for me, but the luck ended there and I have never been lucky since. I have often thought that I would have been lucky to die. After all, life is not bad at times. Indeed, it may be compared to the curate's egg—"Parts of it are excellent". This evening, I took Peg for a walk. I had to do all the walking and carry her. Mrs. Strachan was over. I called at Mrs. Jardine's to enquire after her son who is in Leith Hospital. He is now getting on well. I'm glad. I got a concert ticket from Mrs. J.

I called into the Oddfellows' Hall to hear it but Peg wanted to her mother and after hearing one verse of a song badly sung, and seeing a cake-walk dance, then hearing the chairman raving for a few minutes, I withdrew in modest confusion.

At 10 p.m. I had to go to Gorgie for a milk-pump for Liz.

Saturday June 10	Today I went through the very trying ordeal of having a bath. It cost me 3d. This made it a double trial. A Scotsman was once attacked by two roughs with intent to rob. The Scotsman fought gamely but was eventually overcome. On searching him, they found 3d. and as they sat on his face and wiped the perspiration from their foreheads, one said to the other, "I say, Jim, if he'd another 3d. he'd have killed both of us." A Scotsman is not mean, he is a student of economy in an acute form. "I wasna hauf an hoor in London when bang went saxpence."

Today I went down to the Gardens with wee Peg to hear the 17th Lancers Band. Peg was dressed in white. She got hold of my fountain pen and in a very short space of time she was dressed in black and white. She was very cross. I came home and tried to compose a poem. I myself was not very composed but succeeded in doing the former. The theme of the ode is: A young man started saving up for a bike and when he'd got nearly enough his wife had twins and he had to spend his savings on a bassinette.

Walk with the G.'s and P. Welsh in the evening. Ned's wife is still attending Liz and doing the housework. She is very kind and very useful and we are grateful to her.

Sunday June 11	Last Sunday we had a splendid walk round the Braids and over them. What a splendid view we had from the top. There we stood, P. Welsh, Jim, Ned and I and looked on a panorama of splendour—such a surrounding variety of splendour in the midst of which stood the Old Town, black with the stamp of many centuries. It is a glorious view and enough to make a real poet go into raptures. Today we took another route going south and passing the historical Jeannie Dean's cottage site through the King's Park, through the no less historic village of old Duddingston into Porto and took the car home. It was a very enjoyable walk, especially the part that we lay on the grass and viewed Duddingston Loch and whiled away the time—partly with sleeping and partly with studying the nature of swans and other water birds. Liz is getting along very well. So is baby. He is a fine healthy little chap and I hope he is spared to us. Mrs Gollogly washes him daily.

127

Monday June 12	This evening I went after jobs for two boys—John Gilbertson and John Rafferty. Just my luck—they were both unsuccessful. I called in to Mrs. Jardines, Sciennes, and got a ticket to visit her son who is in Leith Hospital. I then came on to the Mound where I was introduced to Tom Kennedy, the Scottish organiser of the S.D.F. He is a fine big fellow and an eloquent speaker. Kennedy was in speaking fettle and spoke at greater length tonight than I have ever heard him. He would have gone on but nature forbad and Leslie, who was chairman, asked for questions.

Then began the row. Several drunk men began asking the silliest of questions and then later, our friends, not content with "commandeering" the S.D.F. rooms, etc. some years ago, had to provoke rowdiness by asking the silliest of questions. These worthy gentlemen, though each was in his sober senses and one who struck me as being the original of Punch, had as much reason in them as the aforementioned drunk men. These impossibilists succeeded in breaking up the meeting.

Liz is feeling a lot better today and she and the baby are thriving. Peggy is getting very old fashioned and is a great source of trouble, seldom being out of mischief while she is awake. Mrs. G., junior, is still in attendance and Liz is well cared for.

Tuesday June 13	This afternoon I hurried home and got down to Leith Hospital where I saw Peter Jardine who is one of our sick "Sons". I met a Falkirk "Son" there. He was full of enthusiasm for the "Sons". I came out of the Hospital at 7 p.m. and could not resist visiting the scenes of many happy days of nine or ten years ago. I wandered through Giles Street and went up the old rickety stair where I so often went in happy days gone by.

I could not resist going up though people stared at me. I looked into the lobby where Mr. and Mrs. Ward lived. Two of as decent people as Leith ever bred. Later on, I passed the churchyard where they now sleep. May their repose be peaceful.

Then I came to the shop formerly kept by Mrs. Lynch. I could not resist staring inside and hanging round the place for several minutes. What attractive power is this that draws one to places dear to his memory!

Farewell, St. Andrew Street. I leave thee with pleasant memories renewed and with many sad ones restored. No more will I see the kindly and motherly Mrs. Lynch! No more, for I passed the old churchyard where she, too, lies at rest. May her rest be peace. She was a good woman and I would that this world contained more of her kind. It would be a better world.

I took the train up. The S.D.F. held a good meeting at the Mound. I could not get there.

Wednesday June 14	There is a great cycle parade tonight in aid of a charity. There are many grotesque figures walking and cycling about. It is sad to think that so many people must cut such figures and antics for the sake of charity. The parade was very fine for all that.

Yesterday our baby took rather a bad turn just when he was being washed. Liz says he went into a fit and Mrs. G. had to put him into hot water while Kate G. went for the Dr. By the time he arrived the baby was right again and all the Dr. ordered was Liz back to bed for being up before her time.

Mrs. Jeffrey was up this afternoon with the sad news of her son's death. His time was nearly up and he had written to tell his Mother that he would soon be on the water on his way from So. Africa. But, alas! that dread friend pneumonia laid him low and he rose no more. I have to reply to the letter she received from his officer. I wrote it this afternoon.

Liz is now kept busy with these two bairns. She is scarcely able for it at present, but I give her what little help I can.

Thursday June 15	Today I re-wrote the letter to the Cameron H. Officer. The baby is crying very much. I took Peg out. After that I went to meeting at Semple Street where Kennedy talked on the "Unemployed Problem". He had a fairly large and attentive audience.

Today I got a letter from *Echoes* accepting my "Dean Cemetery" article, and returning the Goldsmith one. The funny part of the rejection is where he says *The Deserted Village* is not generally known. Well, Well! Is it not the small touch of Socialistic element that I slipped into the article that condemned it, Mr. Stevenson?

Friday June 16	We have had very dry weather here lately. We sorely need rain. The other morning one of our workers was off work. The reason was that he could not get into the kitchen for his clothes. His wife being about to give birth to child. Moral: Keep your clothes where you sleep.

Irish joke. Bridget: "I hear, Michael, that there is a child born every time the clock ticks." Michael, who has a child on each knee and is rocking a cradle which contains other two. "Then bad luck to the man that invented clocks!"

I was at the "Sons" at night. Tom and Mrs. MacDermott were up. I was glad they came as Liz was not feeling well. Baby fine.

Saturday June 17	"The Lord tempereth the wind for the shorn sheep." This proverb was written about the 15th century. It is strange how anything so far from the truth should last so long. Today it is dull and there is a drizzling rain. There are thousands of school children going away for a day in the country, not to lie at leisure on the grass and breathe in the healthy sun-laden air, but to skulk about in a vain search for shelter. I was heartily sorry for several hundreds I saw in Dalry Road, this morning. The tiniest of tots with little faces wreathed in happiness, all unconscious of the overhanging gloomy atmosphere.

Today Liz is not so well and she has been ordered rest. The baby is thriving and is about the loudest crying baby in the city. I was not out this evening.

Sunday June 18	Today I have been confined to barracks. I am chief male nurse to my son, and attendant to my wife's wants. This morning I spent nearly an hour trying to make an old clock go. I soothed its rheumatic works with paraffin oil, then coaxed it by placing it in every conceivable position but I could not bring it back to life. It point blank refused to keep moving. I have heard of a thing being out of time, but time is out of this clock. No tick here.

Monday June 19	Today Liz is far from well as a result of getting up out of bed too soon. She has put herself back. I have been looking forward for some time to our trip to Ayr tomorrow. Today I had to cry off. I shall make use of the day by staying indoors and letting Liz stay in bed. I gave back my ticket and had my money returned.

My wife is an exceedingly kind lady. Within the past two years she has given away two cradles and now we need a cradle. She has displayed a plentiful lack of foresight. I am glad the baby is thriving. He takes plenty of (lung) exercise.

Tuesday June 20	This morning I went out at 7 a.m. and saw the Store Trip go down to the station, marching to the strains of the Blind Asylum Band. I then marched home to the strains of my own meditations. And I imagined I was in Burns' Cottage and that I was walking through the various haunts. All right in imagination but as a reality not yet.

In the evening I walked along Princes Street with the boys. Later I saw the finish up at Bread Street of the Store Trip. Three coalmen have been left behind. There were several heavy showers today.

Wednesday June 21	Here we are again, back to coal slogging. There was an old ironsmith had his workshop in our back yard. The little girl from upstairs tells us he was a nice old man, but he died and had to give up the business. He had good reasons for disposing of the business.

A northern paper recently appeared with the following notice: "Owing to pressure on our space a number of deaths have been unavoidably postponed". It is very convenient when one can postpone his death until there is no pressure for space.

Thursday June 22	I am busy trying to get up a boot-club for the Pioneer Boot Works, Northampton. Tonight I broke away from my wife's apron strings and went along to Murdoch Terrace where the S.D.F. held a meeting. There, Sinclair wasted his eloquence on the desert air.

Our baby is an awful howler. He utilises his spare time in vigorously protesting against being alive.

Another paper thus headed its Births, Marriages and Deaths column: "Yells, Bells, and Knells". Quite as good was another one: "Hatches, Matches and Dispatches".

Friday June 23	Our baby's yells put me in mind of Tennyson's *Brook*, "Man may come and man may go but I go on forever". I am the man that comes and goes and the baby's yells represent the brook.

What brilliant ideas enter my alleged brain. I thought today what a splended thing it would be if our dear little baby would sleep until he was twelve months old. This would be a splendid idea if carried out by all babies. The Chinese baby lies nearly motionless for the first six months. A British baby is striking its parents in the face by that time. Civilisation!

I meant going out. Wife meant me staying in. Result: I stayed in!

Saturday June 24	Today as the Representative of the Excelsior Division Sons of Temperance, I attended the Mechanics Sports at Tynecastle. They were splendid. Some of the finishes were very close.

Within two years, my wife has given away two cradles and now she is looking for a kind woman to give her one. I did not go out in the evening. We had visits from Mr. Hadden, and Mr. and Mrs. MacDermott. Our wee Mag fought with their wee May. The rivalry in women starts at a very early age.

133

Sunday June 25	What a lovely morning for those who have not got to work. It is blazing hot. This forenoon Ned, Jim and I went down to Princes Gardens. I loafed luxuriously and slept for about two hours. In the evening I went to S.D.F. meeting at East Register Street. There, Gunn spoke to a very small audience. We adjourned to the rooms where I got a few members for a boot club I am forming on behalf of the Pioneer Boot Works.
Monday June 26	This morning I am into the thick of Boot Club work. I will get the ladies' one set in motion this week. Liz gets the first pair. I sent the first lot of money this evening. Wee Peg and the baby are getting on well. Liz is quite her old self again. We have nice neighbours of the name of Moffat. They have two pretty girls who take an interest in wee Peg, for which I thank the gods and the Moffats.
Tuesday June 27	This evening I went up to Forrest Road Registrar's Office and registered the birth of our son whose name will be William Anderson. After that important duty was done, I returned and nursed the aforementioned Wm. A. Who dares to say in face of that that I had not a busy evening?
	A priest told his congregation that they would require to give a little more money to the church. He met an absentee later who told him that he could not afford to come to church since the Grace of God rise.
	Today there were heavy showers. I was at my Aunt's in Gorgie this evening.
Wednesday June 28	This morning, Liz's boots came from Northampton. They are good value but are fully heavier than Liz has been accustomed to . Today my eye had been very sore. I think I will give up eating flesh. I have been lately reading some of the vegetarians' arguments. They are sound. Apart from the cruelty of the cannibals, it would be far better in other ways for us to adopt universal vegetarianism. So the arguments point out and I believe them. This evening I spent some time watching a pie baker at work.

Thursday June 29	We are having extremely hot weather at present. Perhaps there will be a change next week when my holidays will be on. I have received invitations from Cork and Cardiff to spend a week there. Partly through not knowing which to go to, and mostly through not having any money, we have arrived at the conclusion to stay at home.
	"Is Drink the Cause of Poverty?" I have worked fifty-one weeks and been T.T.* all the time and yet I can't get a week in the country.
Friday June 30	Thus the time rolls by, with the finish of today, the fifth month of the year will have gone.
	Our baby is getting on nicely and we are looking forward to his christening on Sunday first. We have today got a ten pound roast in, and Liz makes my teeth water with mention of pies, tarts, pastry and lemonade.
	This evening I attended meeting of the Sons of Temperance. I start my sick steward duties tomorrow. There is a heavy sick list.
Saturday July 1	I have cast off my working clothes and put them away for I loathe them. I does, and I doesn't need them from now until July 10th. What a long time! And then I will have to don them for a whole year. What a longer time!
	This afternoon, I went round with the sick's money. I was tired out before I got to Drum Terrace and by the time I got back to the secretary's house in Montague Street and then home, I felt quite sure I had earned my allowance of 1/6. I remained indoors for the remainder of the evening.

* teetotal

135

Sunday July 2	Oh, day of days! You are indeed a special day for you shall see me at church. Today our son was baptized. In the name of the Father, and of the Son and of the Holy Ghost, he was called "William". We returned and in the evening we had a gorge at roast beef, pastry, etc. in honour of the event. This afternoon, there was to be a procession from the Catholic Church in Lauriston Street to the Convent in Lauriston Place. Hundreds of children were dressed in white for the event. About ten brakes came from Broxburn, including the band of that ilk. It poured heavy rain and the event was put off.
Monday July 3	This is the first of my holidays. Not being very sure where to go, I decided on going to bed in the forenoon. Davie Miller came up and we arranged to do the bookstalls on the following day. I was not out until the afternoon. Then in the evening, Liz and I marched out with the family. There was a slight wind, but otherwise it was a fine evening and had the effect of making the younger William go to sleep. We were home at about 9:45 p.m.
Tuesday July 4	This is my holidays. You would think from that that I had long lies in the morning, but it is Liz who lies long and this poor soul gets up and does some housework. Yet this is my holidays. How can I be happy under circumstances like these? This forenoon, I met Davie Miller and we went together round the bookshops. I purchased Tennyson's poems. A very nice copy but not complete. It cost 1/6 and I am very pleased to be the possessor of the beautiful *In Memoriam*.
	In the evening, I went down to Leith Hospital and saw Peter Jardine. His Mother was there. Later I had a walk with Ned, Tom Dignam and P. Welsh.
Wednesday July 5	We intended, Liz, the bairns, and I, going to Portobello or Musselburgh but it was dull this forenoon. The day gradually wore through without me doing anything of a holiday nature. We visited Strachans.

Thursday July 6	There is much stir in the city today. Cos why? Sir George White is in the city to unveil a memorial plate in the Esplanade, to fallen soldiers of the Boer War. This almighty hero broke the men in a recent strike at Gibraltar where he was Governor. The dockers had a dispute and came out, and our military hero sent soldiers to do their work with the result that the men had to give in. He was asked for permission to start a Labour paper. The gallant soldier refused. He knows how to look after the interest of his class. The workers don't, as they turned out today in thousands to gaze with admiring wonder on Sir George.
	At 5 p.m. we went to my Aunt's at Gorgie. We invited my Aunt and Cousin Jeanie, to our house for Sunday first. We have also asked the Strachans and MacDermotts.
Friday July 7	My holidays are creeping in. Indeed they are flying in. Here is Friday already. I spent the most of today in reading *Locksley Hall* and part of *Dombey & Sons*. I also did a bit of nursing. I seldom escape this little job. The bairnie is thriving and I am glad.
Saturday July 8	Today my holidays conclude. I went down to Drum Terrace, Easter Road under a broiling sun to pay the sick money to a member. Judge my consternation to find that I had gone a needless travel as he had been working all week. I won't curse him here as I gave him enough as I was again trudging up Easter Road. I took the car from Princes Street along to Haymarket. I then went and drew my wages. Later I went to Jardine's and then St. John's Hill with sick money. Walk with Liz, then the boys in evening.
Sunday July 9	This afternoon we prepared for some friends coming. Just about the time they should arrive there came on thunder, lightning and rain. The Strachans and McDermotts came, but not my Aunt nor Jean. We also had Tom Robertson up with his gramophone and hymns.

Monday July 10	Today I have again resumed work. Every morning last week I was up shortly after 5 a.m. This morning I was asleep until 6:50 a.m. This was very unusual for me. I did not feel in very good fettle for working. In the evening I was down and heard the band in the Grassmarket. I came away early but lost an hour arguing socialism with Ned and Jim.
Tuesday July 11	It is very hot weather. 'Tis a much better week than last week was. I am wearying for *Echoes* to come out. I have a short article on Dean Cemetery in it. Liz bought a second mail cart this evening. It is a double one.
	I went along to the Mound where a socialist meeting was to be held. Owing to there being no speaker, a meeting was not held. Grant's wife gave birth to twins today. *Both the three* of them are doing well. I celebrated the event with a poem. I wrote it at midnight as I could not sleep owing to the heat.
Wednesday July 12	It was pouring heavy rain most of today. In the evening, Liz and I paraded our new mail cart to Caledonian Crescent where we paid a state visit to the McDermotts. Tom went to the S.D.F. meeting. I came home with my loving spouse.
Thursday July 13	For a considerable time I have not been at the Guild. I intended going this evening but changed my mind and went to the Store meeting in the Music Hall. Here we just failed to get John Leslie on the Committee. He got eighty votes. Another fifteen would have got him in.
Friday July 14	This is the half-yearly meeting of the Sons of Temperance. Our Chairman was absent through marriage. Poor soul! I have been given orders to congratulate him on behalf of the Directors. This sympathy is all fine enough for a joke but after all wedlock is a very serious affair. A free life is beautiful but it is easily excelled by the bonds of wedlock especially when these bonds are added to with the advent of the children. What is more beautiful than the face of a sleeping child. 'Tis nature's masterpiece. Good luck to you, Lawson. May your wedding be productive of much happiness.

Saturday July 15	This afternoon I went round with the sick money of the "Sons". It was very warm today. Today I received a letter from Stevenson enclosing 5/- for two poems: "To a Snowdrop" and "Our Trip to Ayr"—and a prose article "In Dean Cemetery". He started his letter: "My Dear Poet." Now at the rate of payment, "My Cheap Poet" would have been more fitting. Further on he wrote, "I enclose a small sum for your contributions, '&c'". He was right when he wrote "small sum".
	My wife sank the five bob on a hat for herself. So that what really came from my head has landed on her head.
Sunday July 16	Today Liz came out with me for a walk in the afternoon. We went to Parkers. She waited outside while I went in with the book. Patience is a virtue, they say. Well it is a virtue that my wife lacks. In the evening, I was at S.D.F. meeting in the Meadows. While a young man was speaking from our stool, an old chap kept interrupting him. When Sinclair went on to the stool, the old man listened quietly for a short time and then withdrew.
	Later, Gunn and I went up and saw Grant's twins. Then Gunn and I had a talk until 11 p.m.
	Then when I came home, Liz and I had a talk—Liz chief talker, till 1 a.m. Oh, what a happy life!
Monday July 17	Back again this morning to coal-carrying. What a life of black-slavery. And yet we are told we should be thankful as lots of men cannot get work. Well, they could get half of ours for that matter. Oh, I beg pardon members, that would affect the dividend.
	This evening I went to Grassmarket and inflicted penance on myself by listening to Miller and Richards band. Perhaps the fact that I know and dislike the drummer had something to do with this feeling. I met and talked with Sandie Glen. When I came home I wrote a comic song, "I Took the Prize".
Tuesday July 18	This evening I intended visiting a friend in Leith Hospital. I changed my plans and went out with Liz.

Wednesday July 19	This evening I went over to Parkers with proof of letter and some lines to Lawson W. P., on the occasion of his marriage. I then went to Mound where we met the S.D.F. boys. No meeting, as Punch predominated.
Thursday July 20	Stayed indoors and divided my time between nursing and writing. Sent letters to Lawson and Parker. I also wrote out my minutes of meetings. These jobs took a load off my mind, for all that I was not lightheaded.
Friday July 21	This evening I went over to Parkers sharp. Got the money. Went round the sick and then went to half-yearly meeting of the "Gardeners". They opened their meeting with the usual clap-trap about "filial affection" and then began the business by snapping at one another. Oh, they are a brotherly lot and friendly! Well, for an unfriendly action, commend me to a "Friendly" society!
Saturday July 22	This afternoon, I went along to Wm. Marr's with his sick money. We had a long talk over matters co-operative. In the evening, I had a walk with the boys—the G.'s. Today, John Davidson came to the G.'s from Newburgh. I had a talk with him this evening. He told me about his Granny's death. Dear old soul, I hope you are finding the rest you deserve. If ever I go to Newburgh I will visit the grave where lie thy remains.
Sunday July 23	I spent most of today reading that most enjoyable book, *Les Miserables*. It is a masterly work. In the evening, Liz, the bairns, and I went to my Aunt's in Gorgie where we spent the evening.
July 24 Monday	After using up a deal of time in nursing, I went over to Parker's with the sick steward book; had a walk round and home before nine. We had a visit from Bella McDuff.
Tuesday July 25	A year ago today I sat in the house spending a holiday there. Ned came in and asked me if I would accompany him on a message. I went along to do so and there was a brake in readiness and away we sat and had an enjoyable male picnic at the Compensation Ponds. Today, Liz, the bairns and I met Mr. and Mrs. McIntosh and we went by car to Portobello. We had a very enjoyable afternoon. But often the getting home is the best part of the holiday. This I found to be the case today. I had a walk with the G.'s this evening.

Wednesday July 26	Resumed work. This always is a hard thing to do after a holiday. This evening I sent a p.c. to Peter Jardine, who is in Leith hospital, telling him that I intended visiting him next evening.

The baby still cries a good deal and in a baby-crying competition would start first favourite.

Thursday July 27	This evening I came home in a "drefful hurry, for had I not to pay homage to a Clarionette" who is unfortunately in Leith Hospital. But that I should get away there and then was otherwise thought of by fate and my wife, which latter, by the bye, is just as much to be obeyed as the former. It was nearly 6 o'clock when I got the Leith train at the Waverley. I was in Leith Hospital at 6:12 p.m.

I found Peter down in the mouth a little through being confined to bed. He had just lately been allowed to rise and to be returned to bed was rough. However, cheer up Peter, you are as good as thousands of dead men yet. I came up to Edinburgh with Peter's sister, Mary Jardine. She is very accomplished but cannot tolerate having an "R" in her Christian name. "For her Christian name is Mary but she took the R away. Now she's lightsome as a fairy, and she bears the name of May." In the evening I went with wee Peg to my Aunt's in Gorgie.

Friday July 28	This evening, along with Ned, I went up to the "Sons" meeting. There were very few present, owing to this being holiday week. After the meeting, I met Welsh and Jim G. and we walked home by Princes Street.

Saturday July 29	This is my last day of the sick stewardship of the Sons of Temperance. I have only two on—one at Sciennes and one in High Riggs. As the Jardines, 5 Sciennes are away from home, I have to leave off my call until tomorrow. In the evening, after walking out with Liz and the bairns, I met and had a walk with the G.'s and P. Welsh. Ned and I were accosted by a young woman who declared that she was not an Edinburgh girl. I gave her a match. A strange thing to give a girl, but it was what she asked for. Poor soul. She is not accountable for her downfall. One would come nearer the culprit or culprits in some well-fed church-going scoundrel.

Sunday July 30	This is a splendid morning. I took wee Peg with me to Jardines, 5 Sciennes. We had a good stay there during which time we saw their various novelties. Nearly every house, by the bye, has some novelty in it, if it is not a novel article, it is a novel person. I was much interested in some of the stones found at Leadhills. Also a fancy table made by Mr. J. who is a joiner. They are fine folks, the J.'s, and I have asked their two girls to come to our house on Tuesday first. We had roast mutton, peas, potatoes and Yorkshire pudding. After that we went to McDermotts where we were introduced to a Socialist young lady from Leeds, Miss Gowthorpe. Tom and I went with her to Meadows, there was no meeting. It rained.
Monday July 31	The seventh month of the year has with this day fled, and now we are on the last five months of 1905 tomorrow. Well, well, after all, life does fly away, although some times it does seem a weary drag. This evening I went over to Parkers where I received 19/6 as payment for my sick stewardship, of the past six months. On my way home, I met Ned and had a walk with him. What a difference from former days when we used to meet every evening and have long walks together. Now it is only now and then this occurs, of course. Circumstances alter cases, as the man said when he appeared with a silver watch after having had a gold one.
Tuesday Aug. 1	I was not out this evening. At 7:10 p.m., Miss Jenny and Miss May Jardine came and Liz and I entertained them until after 10 p.m. When they were going downstairs, Jenny was feeling her way as it is dark at the foot, and she put her finger into the eye of a young man who was making love at that particular place. Now as a rule, a young man who courts has something in his eye, but he does not like it to be the finger of another female!

Wednesday Aug. 2	On Sunday last at 10:30 p.m. as I walked up and down our room with the baby, the incandescent light from the street shone on his face casting a weird whiteness to fall thereon. It caused a shudder to run through me, especially as he had been rather puny during the day. He is much better now, and both Peg and he are getting on well. We had wee Peg's photo taken on Saturday last. We got the proof this evening. It is not nice. We were at my Aunt's in Gorgie in afternoon. I did not go out in evening.
Thursday Aug. 3	This evening I went to Tom McDermott's house to accompany him and Miss Gowthorpe to the S.D.F. meeting. She was getting ready to go to the Empire Theatre with Mrs. McD. and Tom came in with the news that he would have to leave that evening for London. He had intended leaving on Friday night, but found tonight's train to suit him better.
	Our children are still well. People are blessed who have children but they are doubly blessed if they have healthy children. Of course, one can get too much of a good thing and blessings in the shape of many children are, as a rule, not welcome.
Friday Aug. 4	Liz was at Strachans this afternoon. I went over for her. This afternoon there was a lady called at our house when there was nobody in. She did not leave her name and I am wondering who she could be. When we returned from Strachan's, I went out to the "Gardeners'" meeting. This is the first "Gardners'" meeting I have attended for a long time, with the exception of the recent half-yearly. It rained heavily this evening. It is a good thing as we sorely need rain.
Saturday Aug. 5	This is a changeable day: sometimes drizzly, other times a cold wind, and other times very warm. We have been very busy at our work. In the evening, I had a walk up to the public library, then a walk round the bookshops. I purchased three books. Cost of whole—4d. If not good, they are certainly not dear. In the evening, we had visits from my cousin, Jean Forbes and Mrs. McD.

Sunday Aug. 6	I have just created a record for I have not read one of the books I have bought. This is a habit of mine—to buy a book, cherish it all the way home, then put it in the bookcase and never think of it more. But this one I have read. It is *Dr. Hudenham's Process* by Bellamy and is very good.
	In the evening, Liz and I and the bairns went to McD.'s. She was gone out. We then went right to the Meadows where we heard Young of Musselburgh speaking for the S.D.F.
Monday Aug. 7	This evening the S.D.F. had Comrade Webster of London speaking for us at the Mound. He pitched into the Liberals and dwelt at length on "The Unemployed Problem". The meeting broke up at 9:20 p.m.
	Then we went to the rooms where we spent an enjoyable hour. It was 11 p.m. before I got home.
Tuesday Aug. 8	This evening we were to have Comrade McLean of Glasgow speaking for us at the Mound. He was detained at Galashiels to form a new branch of the S.D.F. That was a good reason for absence. Our own George Gunn filled up the gap and spoke well. Bob Allen also spoke. Then Gunn again got up and asked for questions. He got some and answered them. Today we have the startling news of a boy who lived opposite us, aged 17, hanging himself. He had been looking forward to going away for a holiday. Pour soul. Yours will be a long holiday!
Wednesday Aug. 9	This evening it rained heavily. Liz and the bairns were at my Aunt's in Gorgie and I went out at 7 p.m. and brought them home. I did not go out later as it still rained.
	While I was watching our mail cart in Morrison Street, the baby began to cry. Then Peg started also. A pretty fix I was in when the people turned round and looked at me in my embarrassment.
	Liz is well. So are the children. Last night I wrote to Mr. Robin. Also Lizzie's parents in Cardiff. This evening I wrote to Jim G. who is in Newburgh for his holiday.

Thursday Aug. 10	What a tease our wee Peg is at times. When the baby is asleep she is at her worst. She seems to delight in waking him. Her voice seems louder and shriller when he is asleep. I thought to have gone to the S.D.F. or Guild meeting. I remained indoors.
Friday Aug. 11	Comrade McLean, a Glasgow school teacher, is at present in Edinburgh lecturing for the S.D.F. He addressed a meeting of over five hundred at the Mound this evening. I was at the "Sons" meeting this evening. I made the acquaintance of Bryce Cochrane, a bookseller in Baxendine's. This is the kind of man I have been looking for.
Saturday Aug. 12	This is the great day when Englishmen come north to shoot on our hills on which we ourselves dare not shoot. They also fish in our waters in which we dare not fish. Instead, the humble native humbly salutes the English lord of money.
	This afternoon, Liz and I went to the Working Men's Flower Show in Corn Exchange. What an array of nature's charming handiwork. The band too was very enjoyable. When we came home we found that our cat had been up to its ornament-breaking games. What a lot that cat has cost us. It stole two fish in one day this week. It has been often sentenced to death by drowning, but always reprieved. Tonight the sentence was carried out and our puffer is now no more.
Sunday Aug. 13	This morning, Peg and I were out early. The weather was delightful. In the forenoon, Peg and I went down to McDermott's. Tom came home yesterday morning after a week's holiday in London. In the afternoon, McLean spoke for the S.D.F. in the Meadows. He is a most earnest young man. We had Peggy Forbes and her chum, Aggie Something, up to tea. I intended going back to the Meadows at 7 p.m., but my eyes were very sore and I stayed at home and re-wrote "Observations on Babies".

Wednesday Aug. 16	This evening I took wee Peg with me to S.D.F. meeting at the Mound. I got a lot of names for Pioneer Boots. Gunn, as usual, was in great form. While I was collecting names, wee Peg was busy collecting tramway tickets. I am the simple tool that has to carry her collections. When I got home, I had in my pockets over twenty tram tickets, five stones, half a small watering pan, a wooden doll and some pieces of red paper. She will come to something yet. So we all will. Will come to the grave which of course is 'something'. We can all look forward to that. Whether with hope or dread depends on circumstances.

Thursday
Aug. 17

This evening I went along by Brougham Street and met Mr. Cairns with whom I went to the Guild Library. I showed him and got his opinion of my articles, "Some Observations on Babies" and "What Shakespeare Says". He said they were both good enough for *Echoes*. I went home with him and got an invitation to come and spend the evening with him on Tuesday next.

Friday
Aug. 18

Rose Jarvis was to have spoken at the Mound this evening. This hard-working, good woman broke down in health and could not appear. A successful meeting was held. Allan and Sinclair spoke.

1 9 0 5
Sunday
Aug. 20

Today I start a new book, for all that, I do not turn over a new leaf. 'Tis a great idea keeping a diary. It is a great aid to prose writing. I have kept a diary since 1898, over seven years; that is why I am one of the foremost prose writers today in existence.

This afternoon, Liz, the bairns and I went up to the Meadows. The S.D.F. held a meeting at 2:30 p.m. It was well attended. In the evening I was again at the Meadows where we had another meeting.

Monday Aug. 21	Well, well. This is a funny world. There is a barber-shop at the foot of our stair. He was complaining bitterly of a very dirty trick that his father-in-law has played on him. "A very dirty trick," said he, with increased feeling. I thought it must be something involving £100 at least. It was that the old man had not come forward with his week's shaving money (3d). As I said, "'Tis a funny world!" Wee Peg and I did the bookstalls and the library this evening. We both enjoyed ourselves immensely. Wee Will is growing fat and is now a much better baby. For this latter, I thank the gods.
Tuesday Aug. 22	This month's *Echoes* has come and gone. It is really the worst production of the magazine I have yet seen. Now at the risk of being considered a boaster, I must here say that not one article in it is up to the level of one the editor refused from me recently. A very sad event in the death of Mr. King took place last week. I was deeply touched to hear of his decease. He was very obliging and was highly respected. I have strung together a few verses for the occasion. I took them up to Mr. Cairns. Out of the seven verses he passed only two. I will try again. I spent the evening very enjoyably with the Cairns. The old couple are very nice. Mr. C. senior is 72 years old but does not look it.
Wednesday Aug. 23	Our baby is eleven weeks old today. He is a lively little fellow. His mother puts him on two pillows on the carpet where he lies and kicks. Wee Peg is generally in attendance and attempts to pacify him with, "Wheesht, baby, Daddy'll buy ye a horsey." It is very amusing. This evening, I had another attempt at the lines on the death of James King. I think I have improved them. Poor James King. May thy rest be peace! I went along to the Mound, but there was no meeting. I have started a boot club this week and got a new pair myself from Northampton this morning. They are good value. 9/6 Sunday boots.

Thursday Aug. 24	This morning I had a p.c. from Jardine telling me that he is now home from Leith Hospital and asking me to come over this evening to see him. I took wee Peg over and we had a most enjoyable evening. They are very nice people and I am sure their acquaintance is a valuable acquisition. The mother and father are people who have experienced both the sweets and the bitters of life, and are now in a well-deserved better-off state. Their son is a "clarionette" and a fine, clever chap. His leg is still a long way from being right and I wish I saw him well again. His mother is greatly concerned about him. Today I brought home a log of wood and left it in the back green to dry.
Friday Aug. 25	My log is still in the green to dry and this evening it is drizzling rain. I went with Ned up to the Sons of Temperance meeting. Today I had a row with our foreman over a base lie told by his contemptible under-foreman. I told Stoddart a few things.
	Tom's wife went to London last night. This evening I re-wrote a short article "What Shakespeare Says" along with a poem on Mr. King's death, and a humorous piece of prose, "Some Observations on Babies". I enclosed it to the editor of *Echoes*. Although Mr. Cairns says they are quite good enough for *Echoes*, I am expecting them back. I have some fine things to say to the editor some nice day.
	Today I found a purse. I am about the only living person who would pick up such a purse.
Saturday Aug. 26	It has rained all night and it has rained all day, and my log of wood is still in the green to dry. It is like a great many British working-men on Saturdays. It has got more wet than is good for it. With the exception of a short walk with wee Peg in the afternoon, I did not go out after dinner time. They are holding a concert upstairs. What a jarring note runs through even the sweetness of an untrained voice. When we think of the possibilities of some of these working-girl singers, and the money that is spent on trying to make singers of the "cult" who after all mostly screech at best, it makes us nearly weep. Suit sent to altering today.

Sunday Aug. 27	"Life's little systems have their day," says Tennyson. What a long day the Capitalist System is having. How I do wish its day were over. This is another miserable day, dull, raw and raining. I had a walk with Ted Carruthers. I took Peg with me. I went to the Meadows in afternoon. Had my Aunt and Cousins Jean and Peg up in the evening. I was getting ready to go to S.D.F. meeting at Meadows when they came in.
Monday Aug. 28	A dirty miserable raw rainy day. I am still pushing the Pioneer Boots and sent for the second pair this week. We have had good weather lately and as a result we take badly with the present weather. For all that I would not advocate continual bad weather as a remedy. I have been dipping into the humourous works of Theodore Hook. I have laughed a deal as a result. Many of Hook's practical jokes had disastrous results. I myself do not care much for the practical joker.
Tuesday Aug. 29	This has been another day like yesterday—rain, rain and threatening rain. This evening, Tom McD. amd I went to the Lyceum Theatre where we saw the musical comedy "Floradora". It is a highly amusing and humorous piece. There are some fine sayings come from a woman of the world in the play. "Don't you think it would be best if everybody would marry for love alone?" asks a young man. "Yes, if they could afford it," is her answer. Another saying of hers. "Oh, no man is ever too old to marry if he is rich." Referring to a society wedding, she said, "Oh, I expect they will be parted by now. They have been married nearly a year." Good Old Lady Hollywood. You know something.

Wednesday Aug. 30	Today the weather is much better. There has been a complaint recently about scarcity of water. There has fallen enough during the last two days to fill all the reservoirs. Thanks, Mr. Weather-Clerk!

I am at present indulging in a treat. It is Richard Jefferies' *Field and Hedgerow*. What a charming writer of nature's studies. I can judge the man by his writings to have been one of the warmest-hearted men that ever lived. He is one of the few recent writers whose works shall live, I think. "The beautiful swallows. Be tender to them, for they symbol all that is best in our hearts." That is how he winds up a delighful article called, "Swallow Time".

Had walk with Liz this evening. Wee Peg passed Dr. for Juvenile "Gardeners". Had her photo taken.

Thursday Aug. 31	Another month gone. I always feel as if that were another part of my life gone with each month, and, of course, so it is. And months slip quickly by, and so does life. This evening I was at the Guild with Mr. Cairns. We had a short debate on "Which is Best off Between Employer or Employee?" I said the former, and we had a rare half-hour. My opponent was Mr. Wilkie, Master Tailor, Shandwick Place. He is one of the nicest chaps I ever met. An honest man is Wilkie. I won the debate on a vote.

Friday Sept. 1	Here are three good rules for reading. I think they are Emerson's:

Don't read any but famous books;
Don't read any new book until it is one year old; and
Don't read any book you don't like.

It has been dull all day today. This evening it is raining. Liz and the bairns are at Strachan's. I went over for her and came home with them. I went to the "Gardener's" meeting later. Then up to Alex Leishman's with his boots which I got from the Pioneer Boot Works today. Bill Williamson also received a pair. These make three pairs I have ordered this week representing 32/6. Not bad for a novice.

150

Sat. Sept. 2	Last night I tossed and tumbled all night through with a bad attack of neuralgia. To make things worse, I had to get up three times with the baby and attend to Peggy also. As a result, I am a bit out of sorts today. On Thursday last, Liz and wee Peg sat for their photograph. One dozen for 9d. We got them this afternoon. They are fairly good. In the evening I was very tired and went to bed shortly after 8 p.m.

| Sunday Sept. 3 | This is a day of rest so I rested half the day, that is, I lay in bed until 12 noon. In the afternoon, I went up to the Meadows where I heard a good lecture by the S.D.F. organiser, Kennedy. In the evening, he gave an excellent lecture on the drink and poverty fallacy. There was a good attendance and the collection was 5/-. This goes to the Russians. Later, I was at G.'s, and had a talk with Jim regarding the Evening School. I think I will attend Lothian Road this incoming session. |

| Monday Sept. 4 | Our baby was recently vaccinated. After the second attempt it took—a tiny little sore on his arm. He has been lucky to escape this vile practice which in its severest form is brutal. This is the third week of the Boot Club. King gets his this week. I was over at Grants, Horne Street then the Mound later. Jean Forbes was up. |

| Tuesday Sept. 5 | This morning I got up under the impression that I was a grand early riser. I looked at the watch and saw what I thought was 5:15 a.m. Judge my surprise on hearing the milk girl's knock at our door and the wife informing me that it was past 6:30 a.m. Result: a morning lost.

I dipped into *In Memoriam*. Each new perusal shows new beauties. The wife washed. The husband nursed. That sums up our vocations this evening. |

| Wednesday Sept. 6 | This evening I met John Logan and spoke to him about the "Sons". I then went out to my Aunt's in Gorgie. After that Liz, the bairns and I went to Veitch's. There I met and had a crack with an old fisherman. A rare, old rough old salt he is. This is a happy home as regards children. The one recently born making the fifteenth. |

Street artist outside Lothian Road School (now the site of the Usher Hall), *c.* 1903.

Thursday Sept. 7	This evening I visited Bro. Mackie, and then the Lindsays re their arrears in the "Sons". The latter has gone to America and is doing well. The former has been idle for some time but is now a tramway conductor, and will resume his payments. I went to the S.D.F. Business Meeting. Kennedy, the Scottish Organiser, was present. We discussed the advisability of changing the club rooms and perhaps introducing a billiard table. This latter is a good investment for a branch.
Friday Sept. 8	"Sons" this evening. I gave report of having visited Bros. Mackie, Logan and Lindsay. Got extension of time for the former two. We are a mixed up lot in the "Sons". Each one of us has a separate cure for the social evils. One devotes a great deal of time to the prevention of cigarette smoking. His cure is a certain failure, at least. Another pins his faith in the Trade Union Movement which is not much better than the anti-cigarette league. I look to the Social Revolution as the only remedy and I claim to be right. Today we had visits from Mrs. Veitch and her daughter, and Mrs. Strachan.
Sat. Sept. 9	We are having very fine weather here at present and eveybody is looking forward and speaking about the coming Royal Review, when nearly 40,000 wageslaves will march past His Majesty, The King. The papers are fairly full of the arrangements. The men are to land in the goods stations and cattle banks and coal depots. The King, of course, does not land at any of those delightful places. The volunteers will receive a 2d. pie for their dinner. The King receives something more than that. This afternoon, I had my normal doze round the bookstalls. Bought one penny book.
Sunday Sept. 10	This morning dawned bright and fair. In the afternoon, I sallied forth to the Meadows. There to listen to Comrade McLean from Glasgow. What a din was in the Meadows, caused by the unearthly blasting of a Hallalujah Band. They broke the elements and all meetings were postponed. McLean's mind was confused with the din. He told me he could hear ever so many bands playing and ever so many men talking. In the evening, he made another attempt but had again to give it up. We had a good crowd each time. It was hard lines.

Monday Sept. 11	Some time ago, the baby, wee Will was vaccinated. He, like Peggy, had to be done twice before it "took". His is the tiniest little scab and is now quite better. I am very glad to see this result. He is growing well and laughs heartily at times. This is a holiday. Liz washed. I nursed baby. Both Liz and I were therefore busy. In the evening we took out our carriage and pair and had a walk round the Meadows. G.s later. Mr. G. is very unwell.
Tuesday Sept. 12	Men's faces are, as a rule, a study after a holiday. Some are wry and some are dry; some are sad and some are glad; and some are not properly sober. Some are talking in an excited manner about the football match they attended the day before, but few are talking about their social emancipation. Bless you, my dear friends, they don't need to, they are all so very happy.
Wednesday Sept. 13	Our wee Peg is easily pleased, too. Last Sunday, she sang to her heart's content, "Good Bye, My Blue Bell", and accompanied herself on a one-toned 6-penny piano. It was a musical treat and no error. She is growing tall and is very old-fashioned. She says her words with astonishing clearness and repeats whatever she hears said.
Thursday Sept. 14	This evening I was at the Guild. This is probably my last night at the Guild for the session as I intend to attend Lothian Road Evening Classes during the ensuing winter. I am sorry to miss the Guild as it is an education in itself. I shall have to throw up my post as librarian's assistant. I went home with Mr. Cairns.
Friday Sept. 15	The Review is drawing nearer. Everybody is speaking about it and in the meantime, nobody is talking of the unemployed which is a serious matter. In the evening, I was at the Free Gardeners meeting. I have joined wee Peg for the children's scheme, one penny weekly ensuring us the use of the doctor and medicine in the event of her illness. It is a grand thing for keeping the doctor from calling too often. Doctors pretend to take a great interest in a case and will call twice day. It is not all interest in the case, but interest in the 2/6.

Saturday Sept. 16	Today we are busy at our work as we get a holiday on Monday—Review Day. Our foreman told us that if he held our views he would not work at all. I asked what he would. He answered that he would beg. I then informed him that if he held our views he would rather work than beg. I had a walk in the evening round the bookstalls. A walk again with the boys later. At 10:45 a.m. I saw about 1,000 men of the 1st Sutherland Volunteers coming in.
Sunday Sept. 17	Today has loomed out large and clear. This morning, I went out at 9:45 a.m. to go to the Esplanade and hear the service held there by the Liverpool Scottish Volunteers. The entrance was lined with policemen and soldiers. The crowd of thousands simply swept them aside and crammed the place. Thousands could not see the soldiers. I stayed and saw them march off to the tune, "Oh, Are Ye Sleeping, Maggie". A rare inspiring sight it is to see the soldiers march with the band in full tune. Walk again in the evening with Liz and bairns. We expected Mr. and Mrs. Beckett up at night. They did not come.
Monday Sept. 18	What an historical day! The Volunteers have been flocking into the town all through the night. Shortly after 5 a.m., we were at our window watching them. At 9 a.m., Liz, the bairns and I went down to the Park where we had an excellent view of the soldiers. We also saw the King and his faithful attendants. His loyal subject cheered him lustily. I reckon many of them who had had no breakfast that morning cheered the King. Well, Well! In the evening, it was a great sight watching the Volunteers going away again. There were nearly 40,000 of them all told.
Tuesday Sept. 19	This evening I went up for Mr. Cairns and brought him along to our house. Jim and Ned were also up. We had an intellectual evening. Of course, in a display of intellect I take a very small part. Mr. Cairns left at 9:30 p.m., the boys at 10:30 p.m. It was a rare night and some of our old Kings got a bit turning over. Wee Peg is thriving and the baby is growing. There is a nasty rash on the baby's left cheek, coming down from the head. The Dr. says it is the oil of the skin drying. He seems to be getting teeth as his mouth is bothering him a little.

Thursday Sept. 21	This evening I went with Jim Gollogly and joined Lothian Road evening classes. We are taking up shorthand, bookkeeping, arithmetic and composition English. I felt very awkward among the many young people, some of whom are smart and most of whom are foolish. After all, "boys will be boys". I then went along Princes Street with Jim and then I went to the S.D.F. meeting. Home about 11 p.m.
Friday Sept. 22	After my daily spell of nursing was over this evening, I got ready and went off to the "Sons" meeting. I visited Bro. Mackie this evening. I spoke on his behalf at the meeting and was surprised to learn that he had already been helped. That was mean of Mackie to keep me in the dark. Mackie has violated the pledge, too. What a pity it is that men, besides neglecting their own interests, further cloud their intellects with that cursed drink.
Saturday Sept. 23	We were done with our work by 12:20 p.m. today. Last Saturday it was nearly 2 p.m. This week Blatchford resumes his plea for the "bottom Dog" in the *Clarion*. He is a marvellous writer. In the afternoon, I took wee Eddy Gilbertson and wee Peg with me on my walk around the bookstalls. In the evening, I walked out with the boys round by the High Street. At the Tron a goodly crowd congregates on Saturday nights and discuss football generally, and the arts in particular. But the unemployed or state maintenance problems, never.
Sunday Sept. 24	This morning I took wee Peg a walk round by the Grassmarket into Greyfriars then along the Meadow Walk. My hands were filled with small stones and dead leaves, the gathering of which is Peg's pet hobby. In the afternoon, I was again at the Meadows. The place was like a fair. Bands, tambourines and big drums and people shouting at the pitch of their voices. And they call this pandemonium Christianity. The SDF attempted a meeting but Allan could not hear himself speak.

Monday Sept. 25	This evening I was dressed and out by 5:30 p.m. Met Logan re his arrears in the "Sons". He decided to drop out. I wrote to Parker to that effect. I then went on to McDermott's, then to Sandie Glen's. Then to Gollogly's. We should have gone to the evening classes this evening. Jim said being absent tonight would not matter. So we did arithmetic in his office. I was home at 9:20 p.m.
Tuesday Sept. 26	Heavy rain this afternoon. This is a blessing as the water at the reservoirs has been very low. Last year at this time, we had three times as much water. Jim and I went to the evening school. We had the arithmetic test. I did three out of eleven sums.
Wednesday Sept. 27	This evening, I finished a comic song, with patter, which I started last night. I went over to Jim's and after having a short time at arithmetic I came home to meet Sandie Glen whom I expected up this evening. The blighter did not come and I fell asleep trying to make out a long-division sum. I am a duffer at arithmetic.
Thursday Sept. 28	This evening, I again hurried up, got dressed and down to Jim's to practise arithmetic. I then came home, took Peg for a half-hour's walk, then went to evening class where we had a good hour at bookkeeping. I was home at 10:40 p.m. as I have a cold. Every night I make up my mind that I will be in bed by 10 p.m. Every night finds me not in bed at that time. Oh, ye of weak resolution!
Friday Sept. 29	This afternoon, Liz and the children are over at Strachan's. Peg was in high glee at the idea of going to "Strach's". This afternoon I had a visit from an old lady from St. Cuthbert's. She was collecting for some fund or other. She collected no money at our house, but she collected some information as a result of her visit. I expect to hear more of this. I went over to Strachan's for Liz and the bairns. We came along the Bridge to the High Street when I left her to attend a summoned meeting of the Sons of Temperance. Here I was imprisoned till about 10:20 p.m. I came along the road home with Bro. McFarlane who is a very old man and has cataract over his eyes.

Saturday Sept. 30	This afternoon I intended to devote to my minute book & do other bits of writing, but my Stern Ruler thought otherwise and immediately everything was bustle for we were going on a visit to my Aunts in Gorgie. We duly arrived there and spent the greater part of the evening. Baby was very ill while out here and cried sorely. He got relief through the services of Mrs. Bremner, my Aunt's neighbour. I did not go out later as I was very tired.
Sunday Oct. 1	For the last few days the weather has been delightful and now October has opened with a splendid morning and a Sunday to boot. There is something delightfully quiet and peaceful about Sunday morning. There is not the vulgar rattling of carts and clattering of clogs, to say nothing of the unpleasant ringing of alarm clock bells. This morning, I was up at 6 a.m. with baby. Did not go back to bed. After breakfast I went to bed and slept about three hours. In the afternoon, I went to Meadows. I was introduced to Miss Lamont. In the evening, Liz went to G.'s and I walked out with the boys. The S.D.F. held a meeting in the Meadows.
Monday Oct. 2	This evening I went with Jim to evening classes. What a rowdy gang of boys go there. They do not seem to be alive to the seriousness of education and they give the teachers a great deal of worry. This evening we had bookkeeping and shorthand. This evening, I wrote out an application for a foreman's job with Ratho Co-operative Store. I do not expect anything to come of it as most of those jobs are settled long before they are advertised. That's a lovely way to work.
Tuesday Oct. 3	This evening again at classes with Jim. We had an hour's arithmetic. The teacher of this class is a very fiery young man. He checked a boy for capering, that kid laughed at him and he promptly took him by the back of the neck and gave him a push and then a kick outside the door. He was allowed to return in about twenty minutes but it was a lesson to him and to the others.

Wednesday Oct. 4	This evening, it was my intention to do numerous things. Of the many I could only manage the visit to Sandie Glen, then go on to my Aunt's in Gorgie where I discussed Socialism to an interested audience consisting of my Aunt and another woman and Cousin Donald. I got a pair of working trousers from Cousin Tom. I had wee Peg with me. I then came to G.'s where Liz was with the baby. Home about 10:30 p.m. Maggie, Ned's wife is at present ill and confined to bed. This afternoon, Stoddart gave Miller a row and said we would all three have to do more work and this day we did more than any of the others. Sweet reasonableness—thy name is Stoddart.
Thursday Oct. 5	This morning, I woke up early with toothache. I thought it would be about a quarter to three, and when I looked, the wee clock said it was exactly that time. I lay in bed and sympathised with everybody who might at that moment chance to have toothache. This afternoon, I was nearly mad with the combined pains of toothache and neuralgia. I went to the evening class feeling unwell. It was a bitter cold night.
Friday Oct. 6	Today I got a reply and a request that I grant an interview tomorrow as a result of my application for the coal salesman's job at Ratho. I wrote a p.c. saying I would be at 4 p.m. In the evening, I had Sandie Glen up. I took him up to the "Sons" when he became a member.
Saturday Oct. 7	It was very mild this morning. At about 8 a.m. it began to rain. It poured more or less all day after that. Liz and I and baby went to Ratho when I met Mr. Bennet the manager, and had a long talk with him. I am on a short list. I think I have a good chance of the job. Ratho is a dreary place. Of course we saw it at its worst. We were in Edinburgh again by 6 p.m. In the evening, I had a walk with the boys. Liz was at G.'s with the bairns.
Monday Oct. 9	Our bairnies are getting on! There is a nasty rash, though on wee Willie's head and down the one side of his face. Old mothers look at it, and with much wisdom, which bespeaks a world of experience, say he will be like that until he gets his teeth. This afternoon, I got a letter from Ratho informing me that the situation was filled up. I have not felt very well today, and this evening, I felt out of sorts at the evening classes.

Tuesday Oct. 10	Today I felt a bit better, and this evening I went to the evening class. We had arithmetic. We got a new teacher. He gave us a difficult sum. When he found out that very few of us could do it, he said he would do it slowly on the board. He then proceeded to do it very rapidly and left us hazier than ever. Of course, everything is so simple to the person who already knows.
Wednesday Oct. 11	I am glad this is not a night-school night. I felt thoroughly beat up. The baker at the foot of our stairs told me to take a "Gregory's Powder." I did so. Through the night, I was very ill with toothache and neuralgia. I had to get up out of bed and pour oil of cloves on the affected parts. Rabbie Burns said many wise and truthful things, but none so true as when he said of toothache, "Hell o' a' diseases". Still these troubles are all in the way of a life .
Thursday Oct. 12	Today my tooth was not the least painful but my mouth is sore with the oil of cloves. In the evening, I felt better at the class. I am getting on well with my shorthand. It is a great tax on the memory to remember each particular dot, dash and curve. Through the night, I was again ill with toothache, and was again up. I put some whisky into it. It was only a partial success.
Friday Oct. 13	It was very cold today. I have kept myself well buttoned up and still I am shivering. I have had toothache all day. This afternoon, Mrs. Strachan was over. The pains were at their worst this evening. I was nearly mad as I paced the floor. I took a tonic of boiled milk and an egg, then some whisky and hot water, and went to bed with my head on a hot-water bottle. I slept sound as a top all night. Liz went up to Dr. Robertson and got a tonic and a powder for me.
Saturday Oct. 14	This morning I awoke at my usual time. I got up to go to my work but did not go. I feel much better and read a part of *Dombey & Son.* I sent for Dr. Menzies. His assistant, Dr. Stevens came. He prescribed a tonic but I am a coward as regards tonics, and I did not send for it. Tom McD. came up in the afternoon with my wages. Ned G. was up for some time in the afternoon. Dr. Robertson came tonight. Both doctors said the same thing about the tooth, "Get it out." Wee Peg is also unwell. Dr. R. sounded her and prescribed a bottle for her.

Sunday Oct. 15	Today my pains are not so severe. Still I felt very tired and remained in bed a great part of the day. Jim G. came up and sat a long time. He gave me a scientific cure for neuralgia. It is: Put a mustard poultice on the elbow. This is the most profound bit of science, or nonsense I have heard of for a long time. Another cure for headache: Take three sharp steps backward. I would advise anybody trying this cure to see that the way behind is clear!
Monday Oct. 16	Today I felt ever so much better and did not go and have my tooth pulled. I wandered up and down the house with the airs of a man at peace with the world for my pains were gone. In the evening, I went to the classes. I divided my time during the day to the reading of *Dombey & Son* nursing the baby, and tending on Peggy.
Tuesday Oct. 17	This morning, at about 1 o'clock I was awakened by the screams of our baby. I got up and paced the floor with him for over half an hour. At 3 o'clock, he again started, with the result that I was up until 4:30 a.m. The result was my pains started again, and under their pressure, I went off to the Dental Hospital at 9:00 a.m., and had the offending molar removed while I was under the influence of gas. It is a grand invention; the whole thing was over in about two minutes. I was conscious of the head Dr. speaking by my side, and felt the tooth being removed with a click, and the engine that seemed to be working at a record pace in my head gradually stopped, and I was led from the chair to a hot and cold water basin to wash the black blood out of my mouth. What a picture a writer could draw of the misery of this place! One poor wee girl of about six years came in with her head rolled up in an old shawl, to get three pulled, and she had to come back again and get another three taken out. Her howls were piteous. I was worn out. In the afternoon, I went up and saw Dr. Robertson. In the evening, I went to the evening classes. My face is still very sore and I can scarcely spit or swallow. Wee Peg has been very ill all day.

Wednesday Oct. 18	I thought I would have been a lot better today but I am not much better, if any. I went out for a walk this forenoon and soon found myself in Mrs. Jardine's, 5 Sciennes. After enquiring how her son was I came away with an old jacket for my work, some flowers and a small glass of apple jelly. Mrs. Jardine is coming to our house on Saturday first. She is a very nice woman. Wee Peg is much better today and is at present saying that I am a nice boy. I have written to Jardine and posted my sick line to Bro. John Parker. I have also written a Scotch comic song.
Thursday Oct. 19	I was about my usual today tho' my mouth is still much swollen and painful. I went up to Dr. Robertson in the afternoon. After that I went to Mr. Cairns where I spent an enjoyable hour and where I learned that I am on the Guild Syllabus for a debate: "Employer or Employee, Which is Better Off?" I, of course, say the Employer. Mr. A Wilkie, tailor, Shandwick Place says Employee. So he and I are for it. The date is November 16th.
Friday Oct. 20	I was not so well today. As it was bitter cold, I did not go out but stayed in and nursed my face. It is an awful feeling. As a rule, I am ever ready to laugh but all this week I could not raise a smile and as for telling a joke, well, don't mention it. Yesterday, I bought *Echoes* in the hope that I would there see my name in print, but no. And I considered *Echoes* as a very inferior magazine in consequence. But joking aside, I think it is going downhill. This is a "Son's" meeting night, but I do not meet there tonight, thank you.
Saturday Oct. 21	Both the "Gardiner's" and the "Sons" sick stewards came at the same time today, and what a difference in the men. One gruff and "so business-like you know". A sickening attitude. And the Son's man, "Withull. Well, Will, what's wrong here. Are you much better?", and sitting down and giving us his crack.

Sunday Oct. 22	This forenoon, Tom McD. was up and I got myself dressed and went down to Gunn's. Here there was a beautiful confusion as they were trying to fry fish on a fire that was nearly out. I withdrew until the breakfast would be over and in the meantime went to Bob Allan's. That worthy man was in bed when I was ushered into his presence. I then came back to Gunn's and he came back with me to our house where we had dinner. After that I went down to G.'s. Then came home and went to bed early. I did not feel well. Dr. Robertson was up this afternoon and signed me off the sick list. He advised me to get three other teeth out. Advice not taken.
Monday Oct. 23	I resumed work this morning. For all that I did not feel well, I managed through the day. Hope I feel better tomorrow. In the evening, I was at the classes. Liz was washing. I got to bed after 11 p.m. Not bad for a sick man.

On the Monday and Thursday I have bookkeeping from 7:30 p.m. to 8:30 p.m. I am a duffer at that. On Monday, Tuesday and Thursday from 8:30 p.m. to 9:30 p.m. I have shorthand. I am some better at that. On Tuesday from 7:30 p.m. to 8:30 p.m. I have arithmetic. I am a duffer at that also. It is strange how one cannot concentrate one's full studious energy to some subjects.

Tuesday Oct. 24	My mouth is gradually getting better but it is like my progress at arithmetic—very slow. I was at the classes this evening. We are having splendid weather just now. Last week it was very cold. Liz went up to the Dispensary with baby yesterday and got a new ointment for his face. It is doing it a great deal of good. Wee Peg is keeping better. To crown it all, the wife is in splendid health. Tonight I sold my reefer jacket to Miller for 2/6. He was up this evening. He is a fine chap.

Wednesday Oct. 25	I did not go out this evening. I am the better of the rest. What an energy one wastes in spare time. Of course, the time, too, is mostly wasted. Geo. Gunn was up this evening with his wee laddie, Bobby, a nice wee chap of five years. Liz went out and my nice crack with Gunn was interrupted at intervals by one or other of the children. I gave Gunn a grey suit. This suit served me on several important occasions. I was best-man twice in it and I was married in it, and now as far as I am concerned that is the last of it. Gunn left at about 11 p.m.
Thursday Oct. 26	The month is drawing to a close. Then we shall be on the last two months of the year. How fleeting is time! This evening I was at the classes. I first went to Dr. Stevens and got my sick line signed off.
Friday Oct. 27	This afternoon I went out to my Aunt's in Gorgie where I got a reefer jacket from my cousin, Tom. A very handy jacket. Liz went with Kate Smith and Cousin Jean to see the Cinematograph at Synod Hall. I stayed in and watched the bairns. Grant was up. I painted our outside door with dark green paint.
Saturday Oct. 28	The early part of today was splendid. In the afternoon I took Peg and little Eadie Moffat out and it rained the whole time. I went to Grant's, Watson Crescent and then to my Aunt's in Gorgie, where I put a new hinge on her dresser. In the evening, I had Hadden up. Later I had Mr. and Mrs. Robertson. Mr. R. told me quite a lot of stories but as I was nearly asleep, I did not hear half of them. I went to bed shortly after the worthy man withdrew. He took away my best wishes and one of my best books: *Dombey & Son*. I painted our door last night and it is not yet dry.
Sunday Oct. 29	Today I am making up some arrears in letters. I have written to Mrs Cockburn, America, and Miss Maud Robin. I intended going to Gunn's in the forenoon and the cemetery in the afternoon but my head was sore. I also intended going to the SDF at night. I went to bed at about 7 p.m. instead and slept the sleep of the just. Peggy Forbes was up with her chum. I read a little of Moore's Poems today. The door I painted on Friday is dry today. This takes a load off my mind.

Monday Oct. 30	It has been prophesied that November is to be a wet month. As if in a hurry to keep this prophecy right, for once in a way, it poured heavens hard this afternoon. I got a poetic reply to my verses from Miss Mary Jardine. I wrote a poetic reply to them. I also wrote some poetry to Miss McLaren, school teacher, Innerleithen. They were the extremes of love verses. And have to be forwarded to her young man in India.
Tuesday Oct. 31	This is Hallowe'en night. I was not aware of this until today. What a change from former years when we used to look forward to it with much glee. But alas! These old institutions are fast dying out. Even the New Year's Day is not the same as of yore.
	This afternoon I went to McD.'s for Liz. Had tea there, and was introduced to a young Socialist from Belfast. Home at 6:30 p.m. Classes in evening. I was hopelessly at sea in the arithmetic. To cap it all, the teacher said as some of them are so very plain we won't go over them. He is a fraction and a vulgar one at that!
	G.'s later where they held a Hallowe'en party. Home at back of 11 p.m. Teeth sore and gnawing tonight. Miserable.
Wednesday Nov. 1	This month has begun badly. It poured rain heavily this morning and then more or less all day. I got a letter last night from Peter Jardine. I answered it today with forty-two lines of poetry to his sister. This evening I was to have gone to Gunn's. I did not feel well which circumstance coupled with the bad weather hindered me from going. I was going to take wee Peg with me. Indeed we were about 200 yards on the way when I had to return and go to bed.
Thursday Nov. 2	Our wee Will's face is now nearly better but it seems to be very itchy. This sometimes wakes him from his sleep when he generally tears and scratches himself. Wee Peg is also improving but not yet right. I did not feel very well this evening. Still, I went to the classes. We had bookkeeping and shorthand.

165

Friday Nov. 3	Some time ago I heard of a prophecy that this was to be a very wet month. So far it has been correct, as it has rained since the month started. It was fair today during the day, but this evening it rained steadily from the back of seven right on through the whole night. I went out to my Aunt's in Gorgie for Liz and the bairns. After that I went to the "Sons".
Saturday Nov. 4	Another wet day. It was nearly dark at some parts of today. We had four rakes to Dalry today and I found it very hard work. This is equal to many a full day's work, but yet we are under the impression that we got a half-holiday. Today I went up and saw Tom. He has been off since Tuesday last with a heavy cold. His wife is also ill. I went and drew our Store dividend this afternoon. £2:13:1. The landlord, honest man, will come along and take it along with some more cash.
Sunday Nov. 5	This is Guy Fawkes Day. There are still a lot of Guy's going about. I went down to the Guild this morning. Dr Williamson gave the opening address. He dealt with the early saints. In the forenoon, I took Peggy to Gunn's with me. There Gunn gave me an outline for my coming debate with Mr. Wilkie at our Guild: "Master or Worker, Which is Better Off?" I did not go out after coming from Gunn's at 4:30 p.m. I felt unwell.
Sunday Nov. 12	This forenoon I wrote out my debate. It comes off on Thursday first. It took me two hours to write it. In the afternoon, I went and saw P. Welsh who is ill. Later I went to Gunn's where I read out the debate to him. He was well pleased with it. I then accompanied him to the S.D.F. meeting. Here they held a meeting for the teaching of economics. It is a deep subject but worthy of the study it demands.
Monday Nov. 13	We had our first exam at shorthand this evening. We are also preparing for an exam at bookkeeping. I am still unwell and rather doubt some more of my teeth will have to be forcibly removed. Today, the landlord came and took £4:14:6 from us. He also took a list of repairs.

Tuesday Nov. 14	This evening we had May and Janet Jardine up. We entertained them with Tom Robertson's gramophone. I came away from school at 9 p.m. They went at 10:45 p.m. They are both nice girls and May is accomplished.
Wednesday Nov. 15	This afternoon I went out to my Aunt's in Gorgie where Liz and the baby and wee Peg were. I came home intending to read up my subject for tomorrow evening but was too tired and went to bed early.
Thursday Nov. 16	This evening I got away from the classes at 8:30 p.m. and went down to the Guild. Wilkie had already got more than half-way through his side of the debate without me hearing his arguments. I then gave my paper which was well received and well-backed by some of the members. After our replies and a vote was taken, my side was declared winner by eleven votes to seven. There were twenty-three at the meeting which is the largest attendance for years.
Friday Nov. 17	For some time the men at work have been having vague whispers about a rise in wages. Tonight they held a meeting at the Fountainbridge Institute where a petition was submitted for our approval. It was altered and will be duly presented, perhaps next week. Later I went up to the "Son's" meeting although I was nearly dead. I took up Tom's gramophone and records. His daughter carried the 'phone and I having left in the key, it was missing when Tom came to work it. This is unfortunate and is partly my fault.
Saturday Nov. 18	We were rather late in getting done with our work today. It was sharp frost and the bags were like barrels. I was home at 2 p.m. I did not go out in the afternoon. We had Peggy Forbes and her pal up.
Sunday Nov. 19	It is keen frost today. I have determined to give myself a rest and with the exception of a ten-minute walk in the morning with wee Peg, I did not go out during the whole day. I had toothache in the afternoon.

Monday Nov. 20	I am tired of going out every night. It is playing me up. This evening I felt more like going to bed than to study. At 7:30 p.m., I went to the school. I had an hour at bookkeeping and an hour at shorthand.
Tuesday Nov. 21	Wee Peg had a severe cold during the early hours of this morning. She coughed at short intervals and slept little. Nevertheless, she was up at her usual time—7:30 a.m.—and has not slept during the day.
Friday Dec. 1	On the advice of my excellent wife I have stopped my daily diary and will now record only more than ordinary events. Last week, we sent a petition into the committee asking for a rise of 2/- in wages. This week we get an advance of 1/- as a result. Today we got nice coats from the Board of Management. 'Tis a grateful country and if they do not realise our worth, they realise our wants. Liz was at the Horseshoers' Concert this evening. I came from the "Sons" and met her.
Saturday Dec. 2	There is always a lot to do in our house on Saturdays. I was home today at 1:00 p.m. Liz wanted out and after a lot of bustling we got out at about 3:40 p.m. Geo. Hadden left his work on Wednesday last. He is going into a small coal business. Today we got our third increase and I must say it was rather pleasing to see a five where it was usual to see a four on the shilling list.
Sunday Dec. 3	Today I had wee Willie out for an airing. This is the first day I have gone out myself with him
Monday Dec. 4	As we get on with the shorthand at the class it gets stiffer. Although I have not been quite well, I am very much better than I have been for a long time. This week we wrote out and sent in a petition thanking the committee for their grants. I have also sold a lot of wooden pails to the men on the bank. These have been the stock of a baker opposite us. Their selling price is 3d.

Monday Dec. 11	The New Year is creeping towards us. I am feeling quite well again. This is a welcome change. Wee Willie's head is not keeping free of those scruffy sores. His mother is going over to the City Hospital with him tomorrow. Tom was Socialist candidate at a mock election. His vote beat the combined votes of both the Liberal and Tory. I was at the classes in the evening and the mock election later.
Tuesday Dec. 12	This is arithmetic night again at the classes. I am the duffer of the class at it. Today Liz was over at the City Hospital. The doctor said that there is not much wrong with him. He turned the Hospital scales at 18 lbs. and the doctor said that he is a fine boy for his age.
Wednesday Dec. 13	I have looked forward for some time to attending a debate on "Vegetarianism". But Fate and a stern wife have ruled otherwise and I was busy this evening until 12:00 p.m. cleaning the kitchen and papering it.
Thursday Dec. 14	Liz was at my Aunt Lizzie's this afternoon. I went up for her and brought her home. We heard that George Cook had joined the H.L.I. and Liz is in a state about it. I did not go to the classes this evening as I feel better sleeping at home than there.
Wednesday Dec. 20	What a muddle we are in! What with wet paint and varnish, floorcloth and dirt, I am having a high old time.

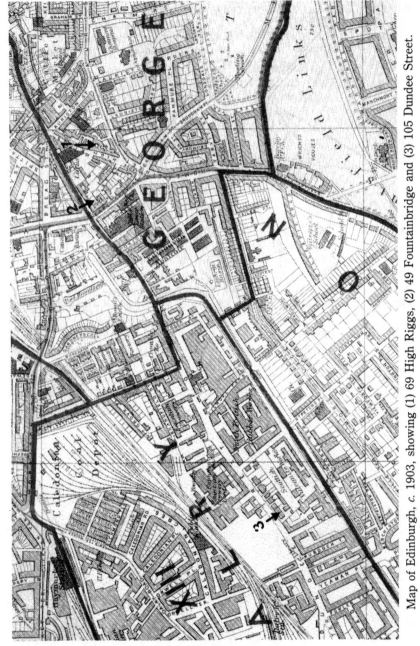

Map of Edinburgh, c. 1903, showing (1) 69 High Riggs, (2) 49 Fountainbridge and (3) 105 Dundee Street.

1906

Saturday June 9	Today I finished work at the "store" coals. I have carried my last bag for a while at least. The name was Morham, 4 Well Court.

This afternoon Liz and I went to Maggie and D⌐ve Ovenstone's with the children. We had a walk through the Kirkgate, Leith after that.

Sunday
June 10

I wrote several letters and in the afternoon went with Liz and the bairns to my Aunt's in Gorgie. In the evening we went up to the Meadows and I went along to the S.D.F. rooms where I bade the members good-bye. Home at 11 p.m.

Monday
June 11

This morning I got letter and reference from Mr. Cairns. I enclosed latter in a letter to Dr. MacGregor asking for certificate from him also. In the afternoon, I went over to Mackay Bros. when I paid the remainder of my fare to Toronto. How they do fleece one, those shipping agents. For removing my box—one shilling: for a little drive in a bus 3d. Add these trifles to the already over-large sum charged. It is mean in the extreme. Later I went with Peg and heard the Scots Greys Band in the Gardens. At night I cleaned the windows.

Tuesday
June 12

This morning I went to Howden's Rope Work and asked a testimonial. He is to forward it by post. Later I went out to Merchiston Cemetery where I visited the graves of the late Mr. Cairns, my Uncle and my Grandfather. Shall I ever look on their graves again? No one knows. However, I wended my way away from my kindred dust with the sad reflection that there are many of my friends in life whom I may never see again after this week.

In the afternoon we prepared for friends coming in, in the evening. They came: Mr. and Mrs. Davidson, Tom Hall, Mr. and Mrs. Strachan and Dave and Mag.

Wednesday
June 13

This morning I received a nice testimonial from the Rev. Dr. MacGregor. I took Peg down to Mrs. Ovenstone's. I left her there and went to George Gunn's.

171

Thursday June 14	Had my Aunts Lizzie and Jean and other friends up and I went to the Guild.
Friday June 15	I called on Jardine's, then Moffat's, Watson Crescent. Then on my sister, Annie, and Mrs. Logan. This poor old soul fairly broke down. Then I went over to my Aunt Lizzie's where I saw my mother. In the evening I again went to my Aunt Lizzie's to see my Uncle Jack. "Sons" at night.

DIARY OF VOYAGE TO CANADA

1906
Saturday
June 16

We got aboard at 4:50 and under the impression that the good ship *Sicilian* was just about to sail, we got to the side to see and wave good-bye to our friends. But alas, we knew nothing about "Allan Line Punctuality." We waited one hour and ten minutes. What an impressive sight. I shall not dwell on it, though, it shall not readily leave my memory.

Such a host of eager faces looking from the quay to get the last possible view of all that was near and dear to many of them. Such a sea, too, of waving handkerchiefs, sending by that means their last tender message to be as readily answered in the same manner from the numerous anxious faces on the boatside.

We sailed slowly out to the lusty and hearty, is not sweet singing of "Auld Lang Syne". We went very slowly down the Clyde. I had the pleasure of seeing the *Lucitania*, the biggest ship that was ever launched. At 9 o'clock, we touched Greenock and some persons with privileges to travel from Glasgow got off here. Just previous to that we had our tea. The stewards mostly are drunk and the dear soul in charge of our table, where by the bye, I dined with a very mixed company, told us we could have cold meat of stew, and we were b----- lucky to get that.

I got the p.c. of the ship and sent one each to Liz, Golloglys, Tom and Mr. Cairns. What a gorgeous sunset I saw at this time. I cannot remember seeing its equal. What can we find on earth to compare with the amazing beauty of nature.

How charming the scenery along the Clyde Banks is, and we beheld the lovely Rothesay Bay just as the shades were casting a cover over its beauty. There are a good few foreigners on board. There are 500 of us. The ship holds 1,200 so that we have plenty of room. It is 9:35 p.m. now and I wonder what Liz is doing, and are the bairns in bed? At the back of ten we went below. The head steward declared that there would be no tea or coffee to supper. Then the row began. It was worth losing a supper to see and hear the manner in which that steward was taken down by a man just off the navy. We went to our bunks after 11 p.m. We have good mates—a watchmaker and barber from Dundee. I slept well. There is a rowdy crowd next to us.

Sunday
June 17

I awoke this morning at 3 a.m. For a pillow, I have my Gladstone bag. I sat up and forgetting for the moment the very hard nature of a full Gladstone bag, lay down with a bang. I shall be more careful in the future!

I went to sleep again and awoke at 6:05 a.m. We got up for breakfast at 8 a.m. They were rising from the tables at all sides. Many of them, including my mate, George Stark, a cooper from Leith, are sick. I hear that the scenes among the women in the second cabin are pitiful. I am quite well myself for which I offer due thanks.

I got tired walking the deck and lay down beside a Leith chap. I had my head on his body. Compared with the Gladstone bag it was a soft pillow, though Leith men are not, as a rule, soft. When I awoke I felt queer and got up to walk about, but I only got to the ship's rail when I had to let go. I felt much better after this, but it was severe at the time. The breakfast this morning was poor indeed. We had a mixture of potatoes and meat, with bread and tea. The dinner was much better. Soup, meat and potatoes, pudding, and then fruit. At each of the meals we have got as much as we could possibly take. It is vexing to see the good food that is wasted.

I passed through the second cabin dining rooms this morning, and saw the stewards throw great quantities of good ham and eggs, etc. into the waste pails. My mate has not taken any food today.

6 p.m. We have had tea. It consisted of corned meat—Oh, Chicago Horror—or sausages, brown and white bread, butter, jam and pickles. I took a plain tea of bread, butter and jam. The head steward came round and asked us if we were having plenty of food. The reply was a ready "yes".

George Stark is still sick and again had to rise from the table without touching the food. I brought him up a bit of bread with butter and jam on it.

174

There have been various species of fish seen today. I went to the side to look at some porpoises, and as a result felt myself getting giddy. It must be a whale or a sea serpent that I will go to the side for again. I feel fairly well. The women have brightened up a bit. In the morning they were lying like dead things on the deck. It is pretty wearisome, too, with nothing to look at but a vast sheet of water on every side.

Truly it is a great thing to reflect on, but one cannot always be reflecting, especially when in a semi-sick state. Still one need not weary as there are always some fools sent by a merciful providence to relieve the monotony of the wise. Perhaps someone is being relieved at the present moment by watching me!

I have accompanied George down to bed. He has put in a bad day and I hope he is better tomorrow.

We had supper: Cabin biscuits, butter, cheese, and tea or gruel. We are being well fed but the tea is not good. Of course, the Allan Line has a reputation to keep up in this direction. "I'm afraid to stir that tea in case I bend it," said one fellow.

There are some ladies singing hymns and playing a piano in the second cabins. The singing blended with the crying of some little girls and children makes a curious blend. What a various animal man is, to be sure. I had to put back the hands of my watch from 7:45 p.m. to 7:10 p.m. this evening. Bed at 10:40 p.m.

Monday
June 18

I slept well during the night. Awoke at 6:05 a.m. What a rowdy crew of young fellows is next to us. They finish up the evening with some vulgar stories, and then a high-class swearing display.

We had breakfast before 8 a.m. Porridge and sweet milk, meat, bread, jam, butter and tea. I took no meat, but had a good breakfast. George has taken his first meal this morning.

I met and had a long talk with a young man from the Parish of Farr, which is the ilk my grandfather's second wife comes from. His name is Angus MacKay. We had a walk through the cattle part of the boat. It must be hard indeed on these animals to come across the ocean.

175

There are various forms of sickness and besides sea-sickness, many of the passengers of both sexes are suffering from an acute form from that disease common in the young, love-sickness. This forenoon there was a concert in the fore part of the ship. There was a splendid Scotch Recitation, well rendered by a thorough Scottie. The love song, "The Sheltering Palm" from *Floridora* was very well sung. The bell then sounded for dinner. We had soup, boiled rabbit, potatoes, and rice. A good meal.

It was raining when we came up again. After some little time, the rain went off, and for want of a better occupation, I went to sleep. I woke up thinking I was in Heaven but it was not the singing of angels I heard but a concert in full swing on the deck. The talent was of good order but the piper—oh, that piper! They should have put him down in the hold until he had tuned his pipes at least.

We had tea shortly after this. Bread, butter, marmalade, pickles and stewed steak or Chicago Horror. The stewards call this latter dainty "cold meat." It is not so cold as the cold shiver I have when I think of it.

After tea, we went to the ship's purser and got a line from him for our railway ticket. We also got from the steward a line to fill up stating our age, occupation, single or married, can you read and write, etc., to be attached to the ocean and railway tickets.

We are travelling at the rate of 300 miles in twenty-four hours. I saw a wee lass so like our Peg in the second cabin today. She was jumping about as lively as a kitten. I wish it had been Peg. But I'll see them all yet. I wonder what they are doing just this moment, 6:15 p.m., Greenwich.

In a moment of rashness, I put my name down to sing a song at tomorrow's concert.

When it was 8:35 p.m. this evening, I had to put my watch back to 8:00 p.m.

Our supper consisted of tea or gruel, cabin biscuits, cheese, bread, butter and marmalade. We retired at about 10:40 p.m.

There was much singing until much later. A ship passed us tonight.

| Tuesday | It is very choppy this morning. We are now in a part |
| June 19 | which the sailors call "The Devil's Hole" and it is always |

Tuesday
June 19

It is very choppy this morning. We are now in a part which the sailors call "The Devil's Hole" and it is always rough here. We are lucky it is no worse. We had breakfast at about 8 a.m. Porridge, milk, tea, bread, butter, jam and fish or sausages. I partook of sausages instead of fish. It was salt cod. There was a religious meeting on deck. It was poorly attended. I counted seventeen, fifteen of which belonged to the "unco guid" themselves. I don't find myself in harmony with some of their views for all that they are very earnest, especially one young man whose trousers are much too short for long trousers, and much too long for knickers. Perhaps he has been at a loss to know which to have and has chosen between the two.

This forenoon an officer took from us our ocean ticket and the form we filled up yesterday. Owing to the roughness there is much sickness today.

We had pea soup, potatoes, meat and fruit pie. A good dinner. After that we had a tug-o'-war on the deck. We were to have held sports today but as it rained we went below and held a concert at which I sang, "My Sweetheart when a Boy"!

It has been rough all day. The monotony was greatly relieved by us sighting a ship which, though going the same way as us, we soon passed and lost sight of.

For tea we had cottage pie, a nice dish—or Chicago Horror. A piece of the latter dainty lay on my plate next to my piece of pie. 'Tis there yet for me. Oh, Upton Sinclair! We owe thee much.

It is wearisome, too, on board. One is always seeing the same set of faces, tho' some of them are indeed an interesting study. Here we are hundreds of miles out of sight. It is now that I can partly realise the vastness of the sea with its boundless stretches on all sides.

What a rare servant, too, to men it is. And how unchanging. Not one generation does it serve but for all time. We had for supper tea or gruel with bread and butter and jam and cabin biscuits.

After supper the concert was renewed below as the weather was still dirty. Several of the crew contributed. A Mr. Young sang "MacNamara's Band", and it recalled many pleasant nights to me when I'd see Ned. G. going through his capers as he rendered it. Oh, Ned! That you were here.

The concert broke up about 10 p.m. After a walk on deck, I retired at 10:40 p.m.

Wednesday June 20

It has been very boisterous all night and the ship has been plunging with the result that there are many sick again. George is again sick and did not get up for breakfast which consisted of porridge and milk with Irish stew or stewing steak, and tea. There was one of the ships crew lost his feet as he was walking with a basin of water, with the opposite heave of the ship. A young man fell on top of him. It was a great joke. I did not enjoy it as I was the young man.

There are few on deck this morning. It is so miserable and cold. I do not feel so well this morning and ate but little breakfast. The men are being driven about like nine-pins. One young man was driven against an iron post and was so badly hurt that he had to be carried to the doctor of the ship.

While lying on the deck this forenoon I was nearly drowned with a flood of spray. My mouth, even, was filled. At dinner, we got broth, meat and potatoes and stewed apples.

George was not at dinner. There is another concert being arranged for in the steerage this evening. My name is down.

I spent a good deal of this afternoon in the second cabin. To tea was had bread, butter, jam and stewed sausage or Chicago Horror. Of two evils, I chose the least—sausage.

We spent about two hours after this playing cards—Catch the Ten. It is still dirty weather and there are few on deck owing to the difficulty of keeping a footing. I did not go down to supper. I had a talk with a young man from Lord Overton's Chemical Works, Glasgow. He said no wonder Socialists talk, as he compared the steerage and the second cabin.

178

As a sort of apology for using the word "Socialist" he said he was not one. I told him that I am one and then told him some other things in defence of my position.

Yesterday I met a young man who is revisiting Toronto. His name is Meikle. He told me he knew several Edinburgh families and mentioned the Forbes'. He ran a dancing last year over there.

At the concert this evening, a lady sang "Barney Take Me Home Again." Poor Hugh, I see you again, with my mind's eye. Alas! you are now beyond the eye of the flesh that can recall old scenes like an old familiar song. I sang "The Nameless Lassie." And shortly afterwards retired.

Geogre Stark has been ill all day.

Thursday June 21

The weather is much calmer today. George is all right and was up and doing early. I got up shortly after 6 a.m. It was very cold on deck. There was a headwind on.

To breakfast we had: Porridge and milk, tea, bread and butter, and ham and eggs. This is the first time for ham and eggs, and there was a loud demand for them.

We whiled away the time with walking about and playing cards until dinner time when we had soup, roast meat and potatoes, then plum pudding for dessert. The mileage for today is 286 miles. This is the shortest for any full day but we have had to contend against a heavy wind.

"To what base uses we may descend" says Shakespeare. I am writing this by a long table where a little band of some strange sect of Christians meet in the morning, and after tying with each other to see who can pull the longest face, they repeat long prayers and read bits from The Book. As soon as they rise, there is a card party fixed on that table. Sometimes two card parties, and at present they are playing shove halfpenny on it.

For tea this evening we had: tea, cold meat, or Shades of Weir! Red herring. I chose the latter and enjoyed it all right. After tea we spent a long time in the cattle shed. Through one of the portholes we saw a little bird not larger than a sparrow keeping alongside about 100 yards from the ship.

179

We then went up to the stern but owing to the smelliness, we soon withdrew again.

Supper, tea, cabin biscuits and cheese. Things seem to brighten up in the evening after 7:30 p.m. Everybody seems livelier. After 8 p.m., the concert started. I think this evening's was the best of the series. There is a pompous old Toff in the second cabin. One of these old swells who, owing to my strange nature, no doubt, gets on my nerves. Sang down in our concert. He is a splendid baritone and made a good job of "The Cameron Men." I did not air my vocal powers. I went to bed at 10:40 p.m.

Friday June 22

I awoke at my usual time—about 6 a.m. I have slept well since I came on board. After I got a wash, I went up on deck, but one minute of it was enough for me. I soon disappeared. It was so bitter cold. We had porridge and milk and bacon and liver for breakfast.

George and another friend and I then had a roam through the ship and were down the stoke-hole. They do move themselves down there! The trimmers are on the run all the time with iron barrows. They have nothing on the upper part of their bodies and they are the slave of everyone.

One of them, speaking to me later in the day said he felt like jumping into the sea. This is his first trip. As he was carrying a big iron bucket of ashes he fell with the heaving of the ship. He could not get up until the engineer came along and kicked him until he rose. He was unwell and the doctor called and ordered him beef tea. The engineer then came, and in pulling him out of bed tore the shirt off his back. Thus is industry rewarded!

For dinner, we had tea, soup, roast meat, potatoes, rice and prunes. It has been very calm today. I hear that the little birds that are following the ship are called petrels. One came on board today. It was almost within my reach. It had a bluish, black back and a dark red breast with a dark yellow underneath. The poor bird seemed to be exhausted, but man, the highest of God's creatures, would not let it rest and insisted on chasing though it could scarcely raise its wings. What was its ultimate end, I do not know.

After tea—to which I had fish mash, we saw several icebergs. Great mountains of ice. I hear that they are three times bigger below than shows above the water. Then we saw a small whale not far from the ship. It would disappear, then at another part of the sea you could see the water spouting high into the air.

There is a concert in the second cabin tonight. The charge for admission is 6d. It is on behalf of the Sailors' Orphan Home. All the talent from the steerage is up there and we are left lamenting. But we are going to run a concert on our own. After supper we had our concert. There was a lot of new talent some of which was good. I enjoyed the concert very much. I sang "My Sweetheart When a Boy." It is very foggy and the fog horn is making a fearful noise at intervals. Some of my mates thought the fog horn was me singing! This is a base slander!!

Bed at 11 p.m. sea-time.

Saturday
June 23

At about 12, sea time, today we will have been a week on the ship. For six days we have not seen land. This morning we saw the coast of Newfoundland. It was grateful and comforting. There are also occasional fishing boats to be seen. Today the sea is delightfully calm, and we are sailing along smoothly.

For breakfast, we had porridge and milk, and stewed sausages.

In jumping yesterday, George put his knee out again. He went along to the doctor this morning and had it bandaged. Later we were all marshalled for vaccination inspection. George who has been unlucky during the whole voyage, did not pass, and was vaccinated. We did not weary so much today owing to us seeing Cape Reece. We then lost sight of land for thirty miles when we came into sight of the Banks of Newfoundland. The purser told George's friend and I that we would land on Tuesday.

For dinner we had broth, potatoes, and sea pie. The latter was very good. There has been a roughness about the food and our dining hall has not been par excellence, but there has been plenty to eat and the quality has been right. For all that, the difference made between the

181

steerage and second class passengers is much too marked. They do make you pay for being poor here. Yet poverty is no crime.

In the afternoon, we whiled away an hour playing dominoes. We had stewed steak to tea. That is three times butchers' meat in one day. This is not a good ship for vegetarians.

This has been an ideal sunny day. There has scarcely been a ripple on the sea and many are asleep on the deck.

There is to be a concert this evening in the steerage. I have just expended 3d on a programme. As the money goes to an orphanage I do not grudge it, but it is a fearful amount. The concert has been and gone and there is a row brewing in the clique that got it up. What a din there was to be sure! One would think we were still in one of our highly civilised British towns on a Saturday night. Many were drunk and blows were frequent. I went to sleep and lay like a warrior taking his rest with his overcoat around him and was sublimely indifferent to the noise.

What lovely skies are here. I never saw their equal. How I long for the power to describe its fascinating beauty, and what can properly express the beauty of the sunset?

I stood transfixed with its great beauty as it sank in the West with its radiance of gold and transformed the deep blue of the ocean into a deeper golden hue. I often in these times wish Ned Gollogly were here, as I think of how he admired the sunsets. Nature's works are beautiful everywhere but here they are par excellence. They are worth the trip themselves.

And so I close the Saturday and I have all the time been thinking of Liz and the bairns, and of my many other friends. Good night to you all. Good night.

Sunday
June 24

A splendid morning! Land can be seen at both sides of us. It is a welcome sight. The men are all up out of bed, but some of them are seedy looking. We had porridge and milk, and ham and eggs for breakfast this morning.

After breakfast it was very warm. There was not a ripple on the sea. It reminds me of some of the pleasant sails I have had on the Forth, which, of course, brings up the friends who also went those sails, and sets me again thinking of home. Still I have no desire to return, for all that. We are now nearing our destination and there is much excitement and speculation as to when we will arrive. Some say Tuesday morning at 3 a.m. We'll see.

There have been many friendships made on the boat and there will, of course, be more partings, but it all goes to make up a life and as Longfellow says, "No endeavour is in vain." We shall go forward to the new life with hopeful hearts and we may again meet the friends we have met. Who knows?

'Tis a grand thing, Friendship. Blair says:

"Friendship, mysterious cement of the soul,
Sweetness of life, and solder of society."

Shakespeare says something like this:

"The friends thou hast and their adoption proved
Grapple them to thy soul with bonds of steel."

The passengers are lying here and there, all over the deck. Of course, this is the day of rest and after our hard week's work, we need it. I cannot remember such a glorious week of laziness in my life. It has been a good thing. What a pity it is that I am not a Beef Trust magnate millionaire, when I could poison whole nations, and move about and enjoy the world and be respected. And hob nob with all that is great and good and superintend a sunday school like Rockefeller.

We have had our dinner: broth, meat steak pie, potatoes, plum duff and fruit. Then we went on deck and strewed the clean floor with a variety of nut shells and lolled about and—well, we simply lived, that's all. There is a minister on board, and today there was a service at the other end of the ship. I was not present, as I did not know of it. I forgot to mention that there were two stowaway boys discovered on the ship when we were two days out. Yesterday morning there was another one brought forth—a baby boy being born to poor parents from Stornoway. Both are doing well. We had a meat tea, and I am tiring of meat. Oh, for a Weir-y kipper. There is a big drinking coward here who, tonight, struck a little chap who is a Christian. We were in bed about 11 p.m., ship's time.

Monday June 25	This is probably our last full day on the ship. We are in sight of land and things are much cheerier. I was up on deck at about 7 a.m. It was a nice, bracing morning. To breakfast we had porridge and milk, and stewed steak. Then we strolled about and watched the dancing on the after deck. George is keeping all right. The crew are getting things ready for us coming into Quebec. It will be a welcome port. We all seem to be jackeasy, but after all there is an inward excitement which, though we do not show, we feel nevertheless.

It is not so warm today. I hear we will be landed tomorrow at about 6 a.m. Yesterday I wrote part of this diary and enclosed it with a letter for Liz. I gave the letter to the Chief Steward for postage at the nearest posting point.

In the afternoon, I watched the men bringing up the boxes out of the hold. They take up as many as six at a time. I saw my old matchbox. It appeared whole enough.

To dinner we again had broth, meat and potatoes, and rhubarb pie. Although there is much to attract the eye, I am wearying today. I am longing to see the place. I had a long talk with Meikle again today. We are now in the St. Lawrence River. There are many beautiful home-steads to be seen on its banks.

Our ship is being piloted in now. Two pilots came on board at 12 today. They will take ten hours to take her from here to Quebec, some say. A testimonial has been drawn up and signed by all the steerage passengers to the head steward and his staff. Collections have been taken up for our serving stewards. Each table subscribed to its own steward. Ours got 8/5½d, I think from about eighteen of us. We are now quite near to land—a long hilly stretch on our left.

It is very beautiful. The River St. Lawrence is lying like a great sheet of glass with the varying colours thrown thereon by the sun. One can only stand and marvel at the great beauty of the scene and despise his own helplessness when it comes to describing it. We expect to see the *Bavarian*, one of this company's best boats which was wrecked last October as it neared Quebec with emigrants. All were saved.

There are a good few drunks on board. This despite the fact that beer is 6d. a small bottle.

There has been more money spent on drink this voyage with about 500 passengers than was last trip with 1,200. To tea we had stewed sausages or cold meat.

We had the usual supper: cabin biscuits, cheese and tea or gruel.

Tuesday
June 26

As the bills of "The Greatest Show on Earth" put it, "We have arrived." We steamed slowly into Quebec harbour shortly after 2 a.m. ship time. I was up and had a look from the deck at the place, and I's here. We are at the entrance of one of earth's greatest countries. Well done, *Sicilian*. You have worked well and now your great throbbing engines are at rest. Well they do deserve the rest. Especially as your best day's work, 311 miles, was done on the day of rest, Sunday.

We got off the ship at about 6.10 a.m. after having a breakfast of stewed steak, bread and tea. We had to walk about half a mile when we were told to go back again for our bags. We then had to go through various forms of changing tickets. Then have our baggage passed by the customs officers. They did not open the boxes nor bags.

Then we were taken in a bus to a miserable-looking place where we were told that the ferry boat would take us to the Grand Trunk station at 12:35 p.m. At this time, it was a little after 9 a.m. Jim Reid, Dod and I then wandered about the streets—dirty places with wooden paving and an uneven roadway of various substances.

It was very warm and we were rather sick of the whole business. I sent post cards to Liz, Mr. Stoddard and my Aunt Lizzie. We lolled about the quay and then were taken down by the river steamer to the station. When we embarked several of our number were drunk. The majority of the people I saw in Quebec are French and nearly all the business is done in French.

We went into the train at 1:15 p.m. It is one of those trains that are twice stopped by the same cow being on the line. The scenery, of course, is lovely. We stopped at numerous stations and at Point Levi were told to take ten minutes for refreshments.

At this place, we are charged ten cents for a cup of tea and the same sum for a sandwich. We were kept standing about this outlandish place for fully an hour. One goes about here asking questions and getting vague answers. Nobody seems to know anything about their own business. We are still among the French people.

We arrived at Montreal at about 8 p.m. We went with Jim Reid and found his friend. Jim got settled in a job. We had a walk after having a sandwich and a cup of tea. We saw the Windsor, the largest hotel in Canada.

We left with the 10:30 a.m. train for Toronto. There are plenty of jobs in Montreal. This train is stuffy hot. We put our bags on seats and thought that by that means we had guaranteed them. When we looked around again, George's bag was shifted and his seat occupied. This all-night train is a great deal behind that of the old country. But of course, it is the "new" we are in now.

One very funny incident occurred. On a seat that can hold three persons lay a long chap with an "I'm alright air." Just as the train was moving, a dead drunk man was carried in. This fellow was told to get up and make room for the drunk. What an expression of anger was his. He sat upright and did a bit of swearing on his own. Of course, he could not object.

The old chap who took George's seat spoke to the conductor about bringing the fellow out. "I can't keep him out, Boss, when he has got a ticket," was the reply, and old steal-the-seat sang dumb!

It has been a wearisome ride looking out into the inky darkness, or going to sleep for ten minutes at a time in an awkward position and being suddenly wakened by the clanging of the big bell attached to our or some passing engine.

It is now 3:30 a.m. and the day is breaking, thus breaking the monotony by allowing one to see the fields. At about 7 a.m. we landed in Toronto finally. It was a weary ride and we were thankful to get out feet on the platform. We were met by the usual "friends" in search of lodgers. We politely and firmly declined.

We met Dod's brother who took us with the car to the home of Mrs. Forbes. Arrived here, I found that there was no room for me, but I got a room on the other side of the street. I will get my meals from Forbes'. I am not favourably impressed with Toronto. Everything is so unfinished. Many of the streets are like ploughed fields.

In the afternoon, I went over to the Canada Iron Works in search of a job. No men required. It was very hot today.

Thursday
June 28

George Stark and I went out in search of work this morning. I had a talk with an attendant at the Post Office. He was an Aberdonian. We then went again on the search, and I got a job at a big iron works named Massey-Harris Co. Ltd. This is the biggest sweating firm in Toronto but I must work and I started today at 1 p.m.

The work is hot and warm and as a result I sweated a good deal.

Friday
June 29

Yesterday I got a letter and sent a reply to Liz. Today I was at work at 7 a.m. I did sweat some.

In the evening I was dead tired and spent the evening resting. It was very warm today. 92° in the shade.

Saturday
June 30

Mr Forbes and I went out in the afternoon. He showed me many places of interest and many pubs.

CANADIAN EPILOGUE

My father came to Canada in June 1906 by himself. He left his wife, Elizabeth, and daughter Meg, and son William, in Edinburgh. He came on board *The Sicilian*, an Allan's Line vessel. George Stark, a cooper from Leith, was one of my father's cabin-mates.

My dad mentions using his Gladstone bag for a pillow, and his overcoat for a cover at night. So there weren't many frills for the immigrants.

George Stark went to board in the west end of Toronto with Mr and Mrs Forbes, friends of my parents from Edinburgh. They didn't have room for my father, so he roomed across the street but had his meals with the Forbes.

His first job was with Massey-Harris Limited, manufacturers of farm implements. He mentions sweating a good deal, but does not say just what type of work he had. He seemed to get along well enough, but was very lonesome for his wife and children.

Taking in boarders was one way that women could contribute to the household purse. It would be a back-breaking job, but some of those women weren't generous. Mrs Forbes used to give her boarders half an egg to their meal. Mr John Stark once asked her if half-a-hen laid it!

Shortly after he came to Toronto my father made a good friend of Mr Vincent Bottoms. Mr Bottoms was wearing the white bow, a mark of a temperance association, when my father stopped him on the street and spoke to him. Mr Bottoms was a machinist who worked at Christie, Brown & Company, biscuit manufacturers. He had many interests. Photography was one, and most of the pictures taken of the Andersons in those early years in Canada were Mr Bottom's work. He and his wife have passed away now, as have our parents, but our families are still friends. My dad also made friends with the Stark boys. George had been with him on the ship, and Jim and John were already in Canada. Mr Jim Stark eventually married "Mary". Their daughter, Isabel, was a friend of my sister, Rheta, from the time they were children. Our family still keeps in contact with Isabel's children.

I once asked Mrs. Stark how much her husband had paid to come to Canada. She replied that he came under a scheme and had paid five pounds for his fare.

My mother came to Canada with the two children in 1907. The first house they had in Toronto was a shack. They moved it three blocks to a new location at the back of a property on which a more sturdy house was going to be built. The shack had cost $30.

That shack wasn't the only one in the vicinity. One Christmas, someone from a relief agency came around to the people during the holiday season. When the lady came into our house, she remarked that

189

my parents were well off because there was blue wall-paper on the walls! Eventually, my parents lived in at least two houses in the west end of Toronto.

James Cook, named for our maternal grandfather, was born in 1908. Mother said that she had to melt snow to bathe Jim for his first wash after he was born. William, aged 4½, died of diphtheria in 1910. That was a very difficult and sorrowful time for my parents. They had been the only members of their family to emigrate, and while they had friends, they must have missed family at a time like that. Rheta Elizabeth was born while my parents were in the west end.

I don't know the reason for the move, but they came to 78 Empire Avenue in the east end of the city, and that is where the twins, Fred and George, were born in 1913. From 78 Empire Avenue, they moved to Cedarvale Avenue to a sand-block house which my father built. Cedarvale was far from the city and its amenities. My father had to walk a long way from the end of the street-car line to the house on Cedarvale. A second set of twins was born there. They died at birth. One of the most poignant things I know about my parents was that upon the death of those two babies, my father came home from work one day with two small, white boxes. He carried the two children in them back down to the undertaker's on Danforth Avenue. I know nothing of the details of their burial. Llewellyn Francis was born on Cedarvale Avenue in 1917.

My mother had no water or electricity in that small house. She walked up to the next block to get water from a well. The owner of the well closed his gate at a certain time each evening. One night, mother went for water and the gate was closed. The man wouldn't allow her in. I can imagine what she said to him with her Welsh tongue! The next day my father saw to it that someone dug a well for their own use in the backyard. It was on Cedarvale, too, that my father had typhoid fever. The doctor told mother to feed my dad custards and cream soups. Actually, he should have had very little to eat, and then clear bouillon. That is the only bill that my mother never paid. "I could have lost your father that time," she once said to me. As a result of the typhoid, my father had to shave off his moustache. He became a whole new person! My parents returned to Empire Avenue, this time to number 27, and there in 1919 I was born.

Although my father didn't change his job often, he did move around a little. Often he would have taken a chance on a job which didn't pay well, but had the prospects of doing so, but he didn't because of his family responsibilities. It seems to me that he worked in the capacity of a watchman most often. This involved long hours, and 7-days-per-week work. Once he worked in the Confederation Life building. He put in an 84-hour week there for $22. I think the only reason that he could endure those long hours was the fact that he liked to read, and he always had a squib of pencil in his pocket for writing. The pencil fitted into his vest pocket, so you know how long it was.

After much study, my dad obtained his fourth-class stationary engineer's papers, then his third-class. Knowing what a difficult subject mathematics was for him, it was a tremendous achievement. He worked for Stewart Hartshorne's, manufacturers of rollers for window blinds; Gooderham & Worts, distillers; Woods Manufacturing Company, manufacturers of wheat bags at the time, and his last job was with The Belle Ewart Ice and Coal Company. He was engineer there. Although households were gradually getting electric refrigerators about this time, we didn't. With their ethical standards, my parents said that as long as my father made his living making ice, we should have an ice box.

My father wasn't feeling well one day in November 1942. My mother insisted that they go to the doctor's that evening, and the next day for the first time that I ever remember, my father didn't go to work. He was in bed reading Eric Knight's *This Above All*, and my mother kept going up and down the stairs to see how he was. "Would you please stay downstairs so I can finish this book?" Well, the dear soul never did. He had a heart attack in the early evening, and died then. Luckily, I had just come home from work, and was able to get the doctor who had seen him the night before. So the doctor was with him when he passed away.

Besides working every day, my father worked shifts. Night school was an important part of his life in Edinburgh but he just didn't have the time to attend classes when he was in Toronto. This meant, too, that he didn't have the time to spend with his family that he should have. He rarely ate a meal with us.

My father had a hankering to be a salesman. He was a great believer in fraternal organisations that would care for the sick and those in need. He and my mother belonged to the *Independent Order of Foresters* which had sickness insurance as well as death benefits. My dad persuaded so many people to join the *Foresters* that he won a gold Waltham watch for himself, and then another for my mother.

When he worked for the Belle Ewart, he wanted to leave the job as stationary engineer, and sell bags of coke to small grocery stores. That would have meant working on a commission, and he did **not** change his job because of the uncertainty of money. My father worked all through the depression of the late '20s and early '30s. He didn't make a lot of money, but he worked regularly. He belonged to the Brotherhood at our church, and each year would give a talk on Robbie Burns, his favourite poet. He held Robert Fergusson in high regard as well.

My dad had a soft voice, and his English was excellent. Someone once corrected something that he said. With no malice whatsoever, he gently showed her where he had been right and she was wrong. I don't know how my father would have managed without reading. Because of his working hours, he didn't go to the library as he seemed to in Edinburgh, but he knew all the second-hand book stores on our end of Queen Street. In those days, he got $2 per week pocket money, so he rarely paid more than 25c for a book. Mostly they were 10c. My mother bought him new books, though. And it was a family joke. "No point in buying dad a book for Christmas. He already has one." He remained a Socialist all his days, and was very interested in the formation of the Cooperative Commonwealth Federation (now the New Democratic Party), a socialist party in Canada.

In 1937, my parents had a holiday in Britain. The highlight of it all was visiting Rev. David Stewart, of Currie Kirk, whom he had known as a boy. I visited Rev. Stewart later, and he told me that the part of Edinburgh where my father had been brought up was called "'The Happy Land' because there wasn't a happy thing in it." My mother went into a chronic-care hospital in 1953, and died there in 1959. Our brother, George, died the day after mother. Jim, the eldest brother, died in January of this year. So there are five of us now—two boys and three girls. We have about a dozen nieces and nephews, some great-nieces and one great-great nephew. One grandson is called William Anderson and one great-grandson the same. There are a number of teachers in the midst, and one chartered accountant.

Llewellyn has established a prize in honour of our parents at the elementary school that a number of us attended. It is the *William and Elizabeth Ann Anderson Prize*. It was Llew's project started to celebrate Canada's centennial in 1967. The citation reads:

> Awarded each year to the boy and girl of
> the graduation class of Queen Alexandra
> School whose scholastic achievement,
> leadership qualities and sense of
> responsibility to their school and
> community are outstanding.

I'm not sure how we would have fared if our parents had stayed in Great Britain, but I think we have done well in Canada. Our parents set us a good example, and the least we can do is try to be like them.

Olwen Anderson

February 21, 1986